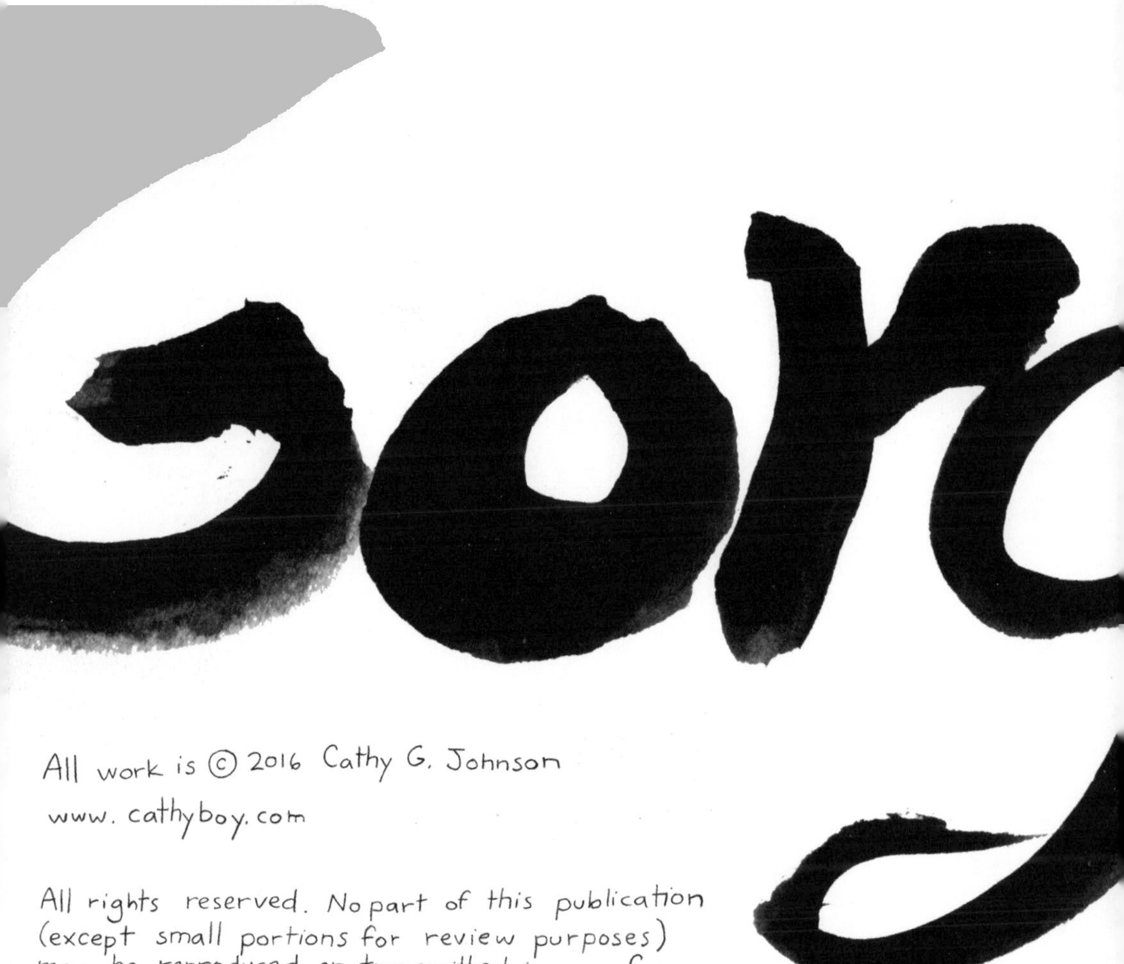

Published by Koyama Press
www.koyamapress.com

First edition: May 2016

ISBN: 978-1-927668-27-6

Printed in China

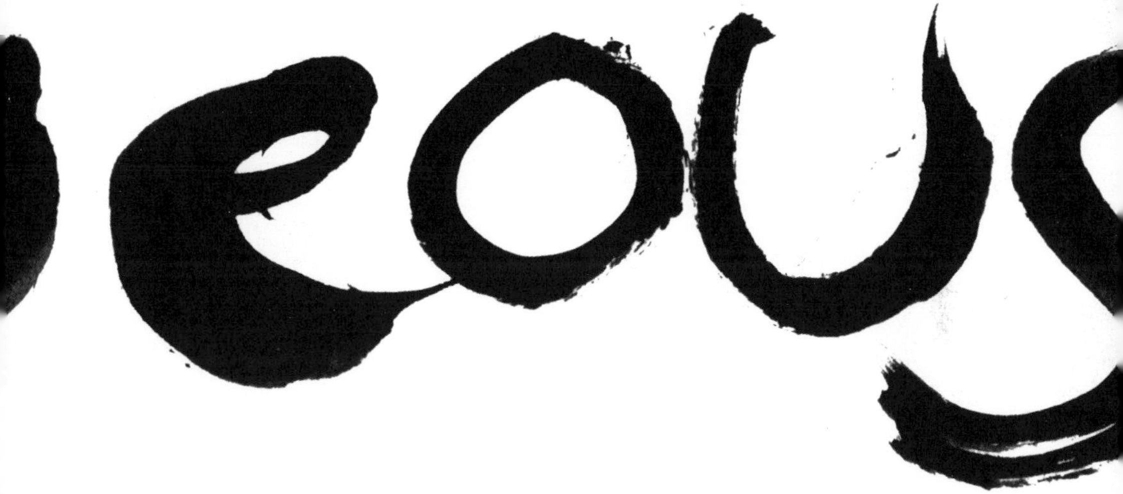

CATHY G. JOHNSON

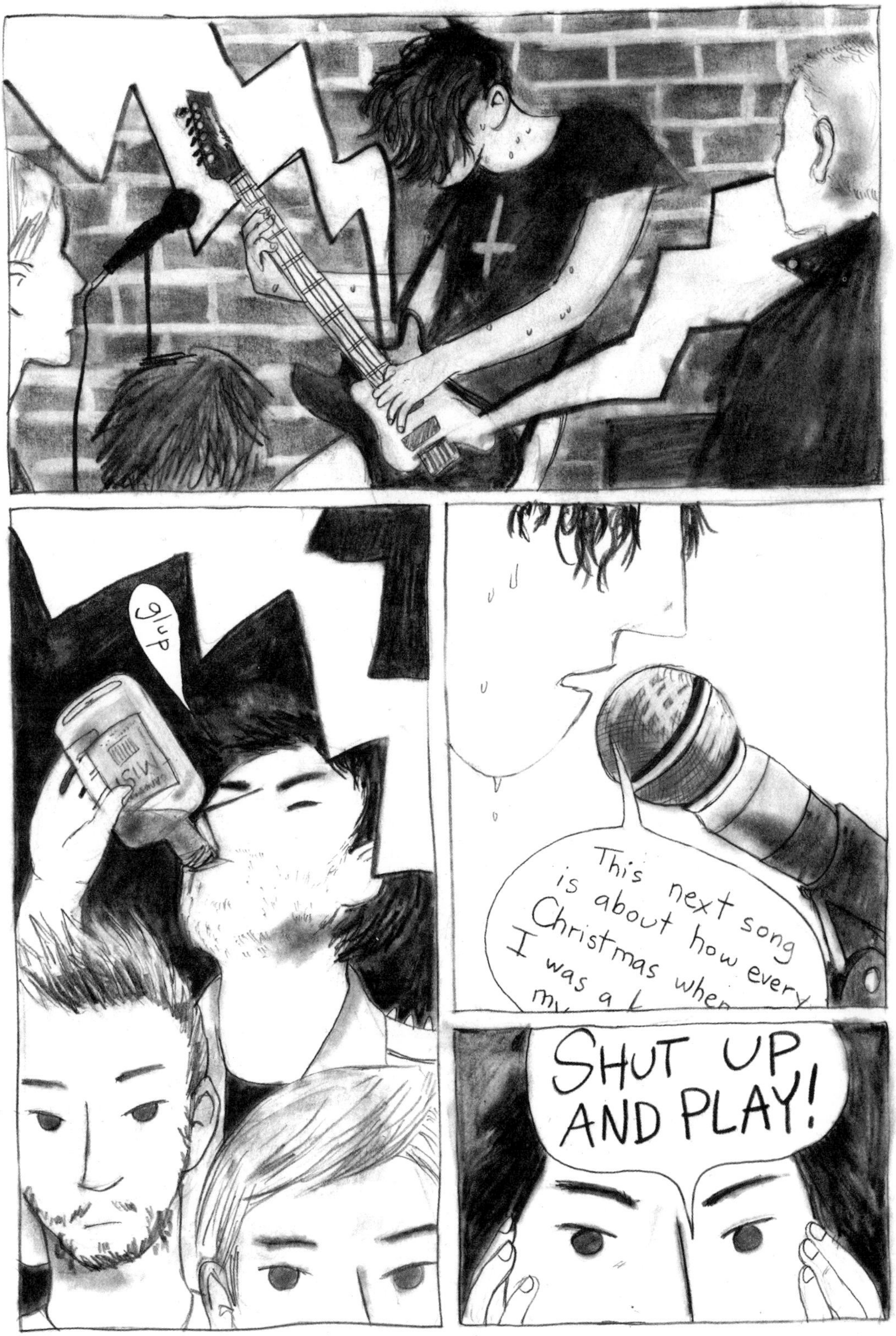
glup
This next song is about how every Christmas when I was a
SHUT UP AND PLAY!

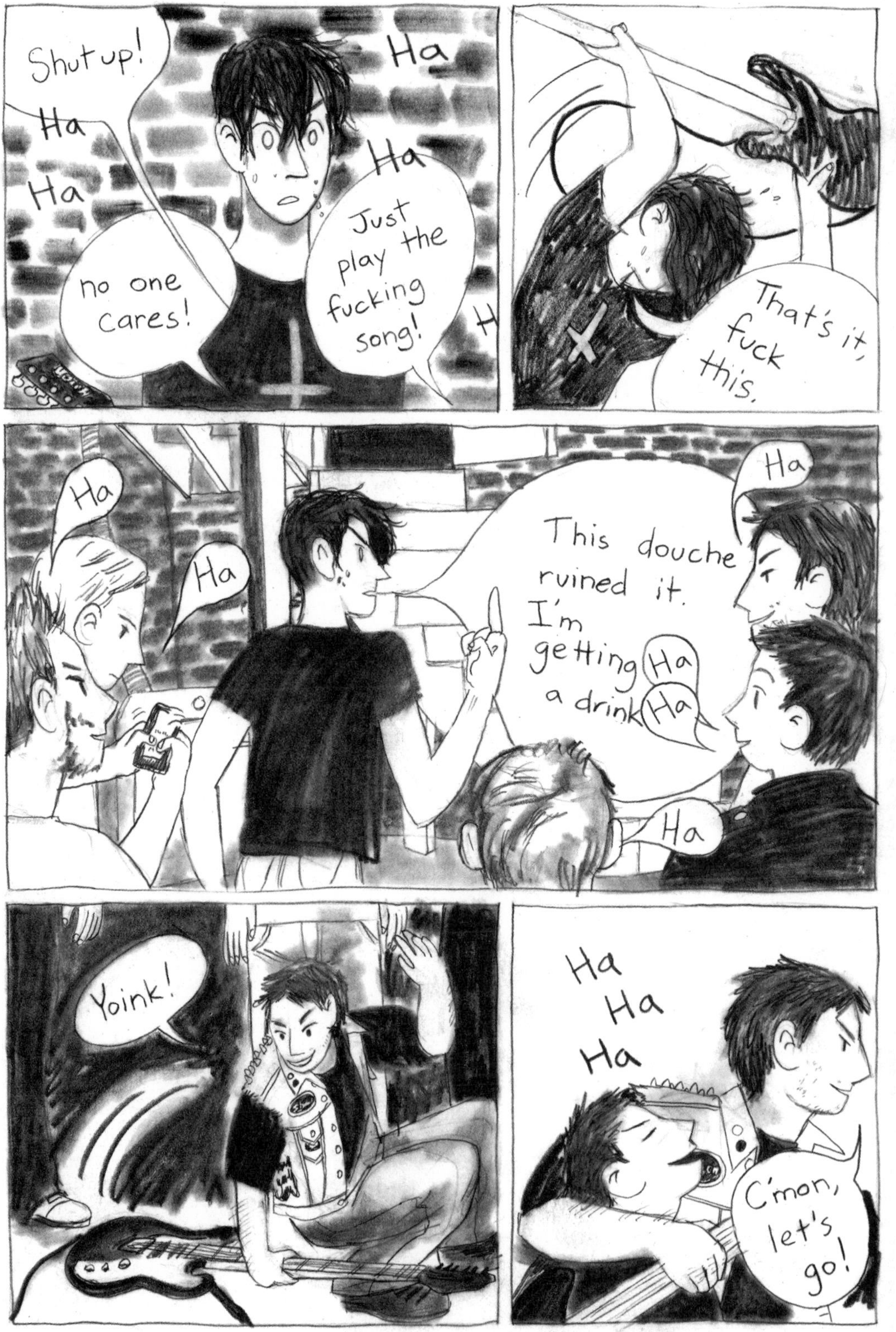
Shut up!
Ha
Ha
Ha
Ha
no one cares!
Just play the fucking song!
That's it, fuck this.
Ha
Ha
This douche ruined it. I'm getting a drink
Ha
Ha
Ha
Ha
Ha
Yoink!
Ha
Ha
Ha
C'mon, let's go!

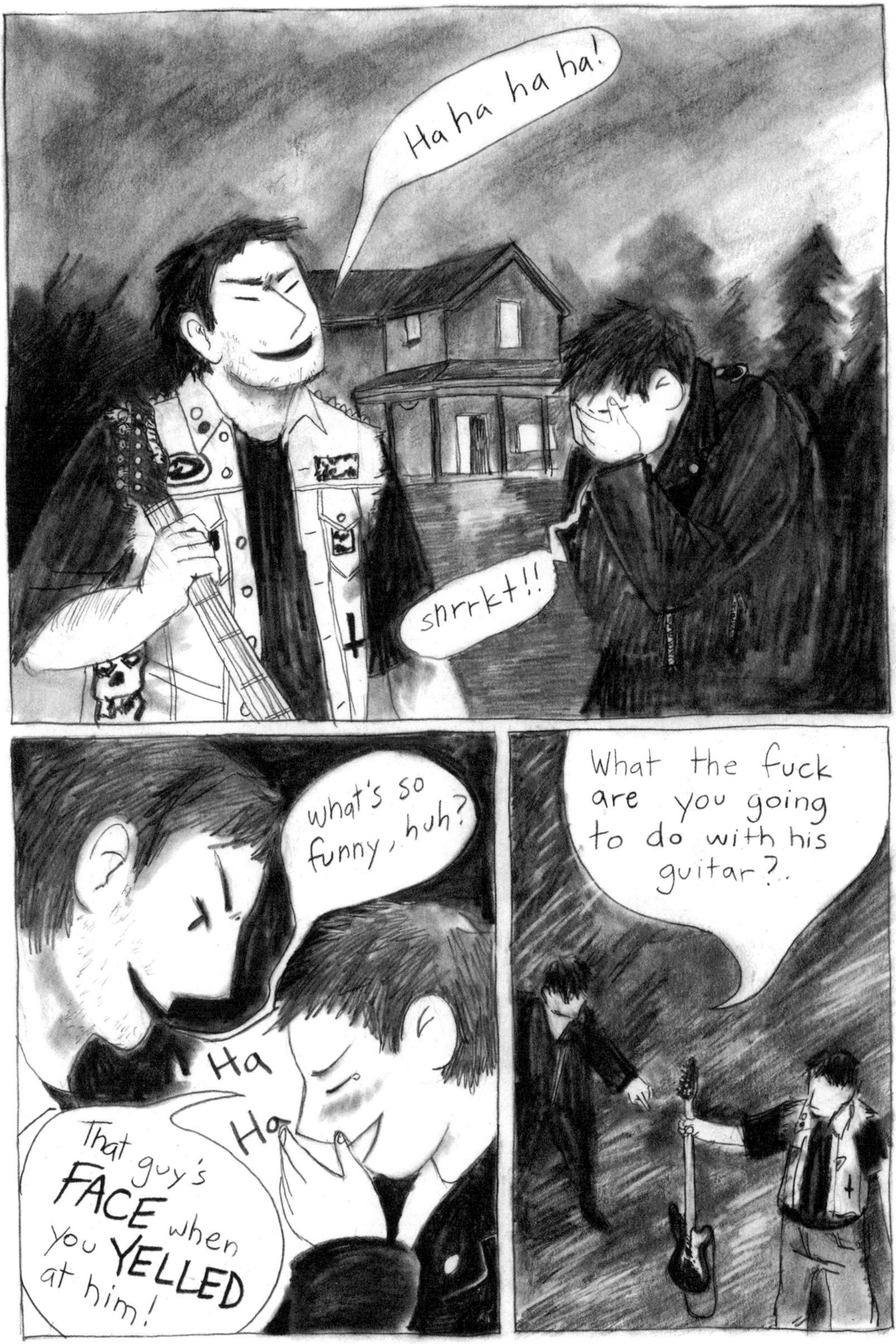
Ha ha ha ha!
shrrkt!!
what's so funny, huh?
Ha
Ha
That guy's FACE when you YELLED at him!
What the fuck are you going to do with his guitar?..

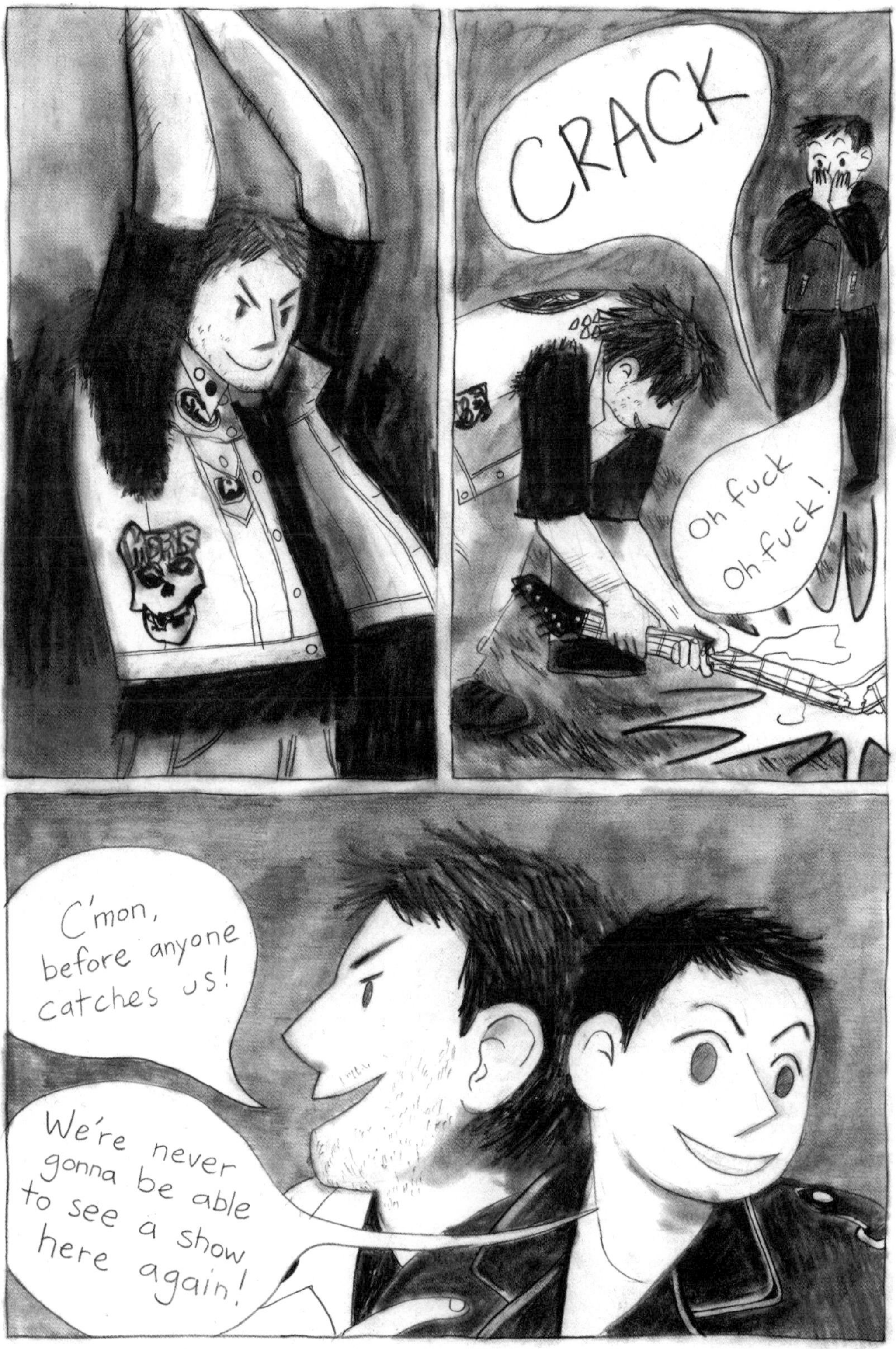
CRACK
Oh fuck Oh fuck!
C'mon, before anyone catches us!
We're never gonna be able to see a show here again!

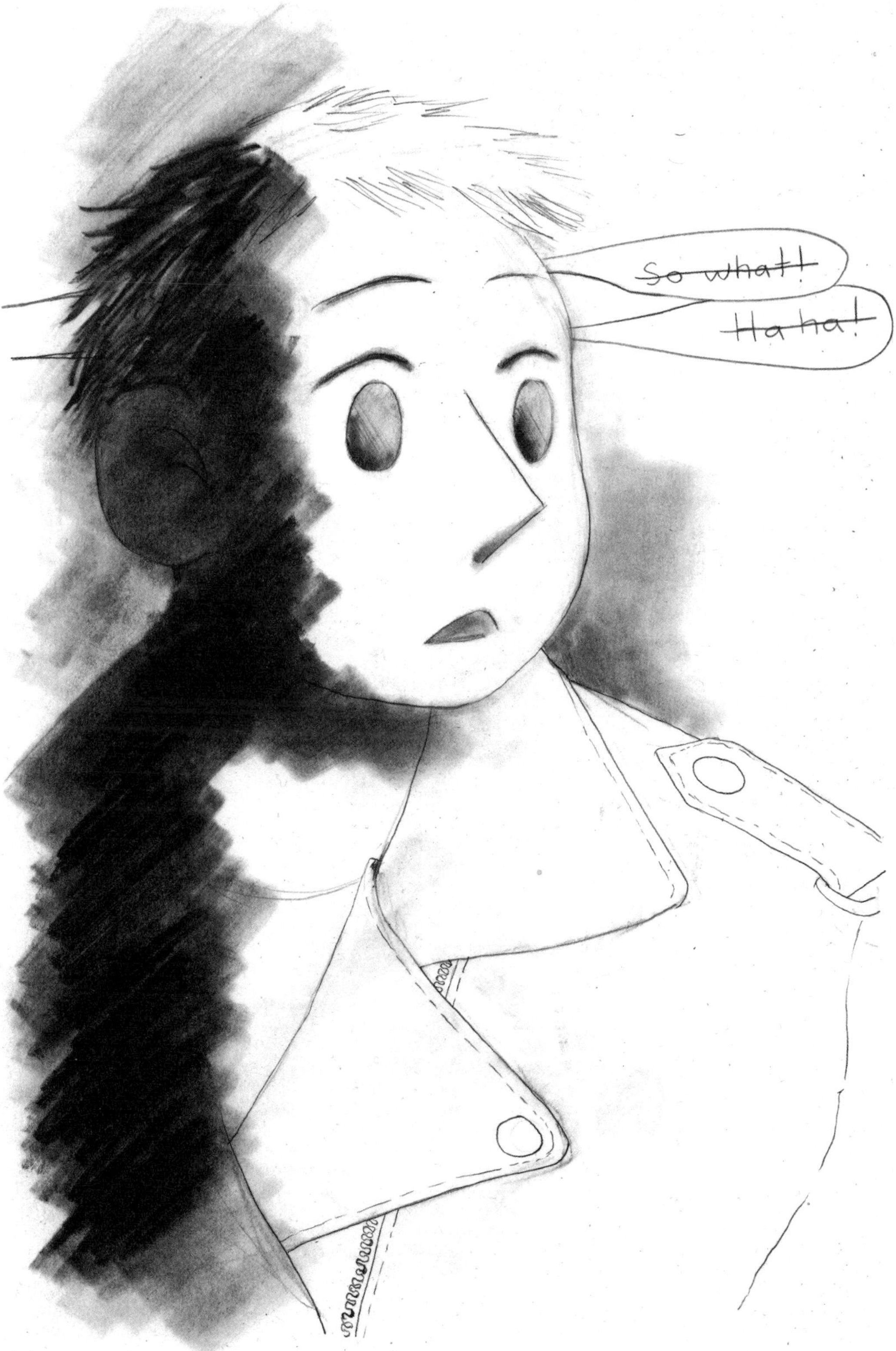
So what!
Ha ha!

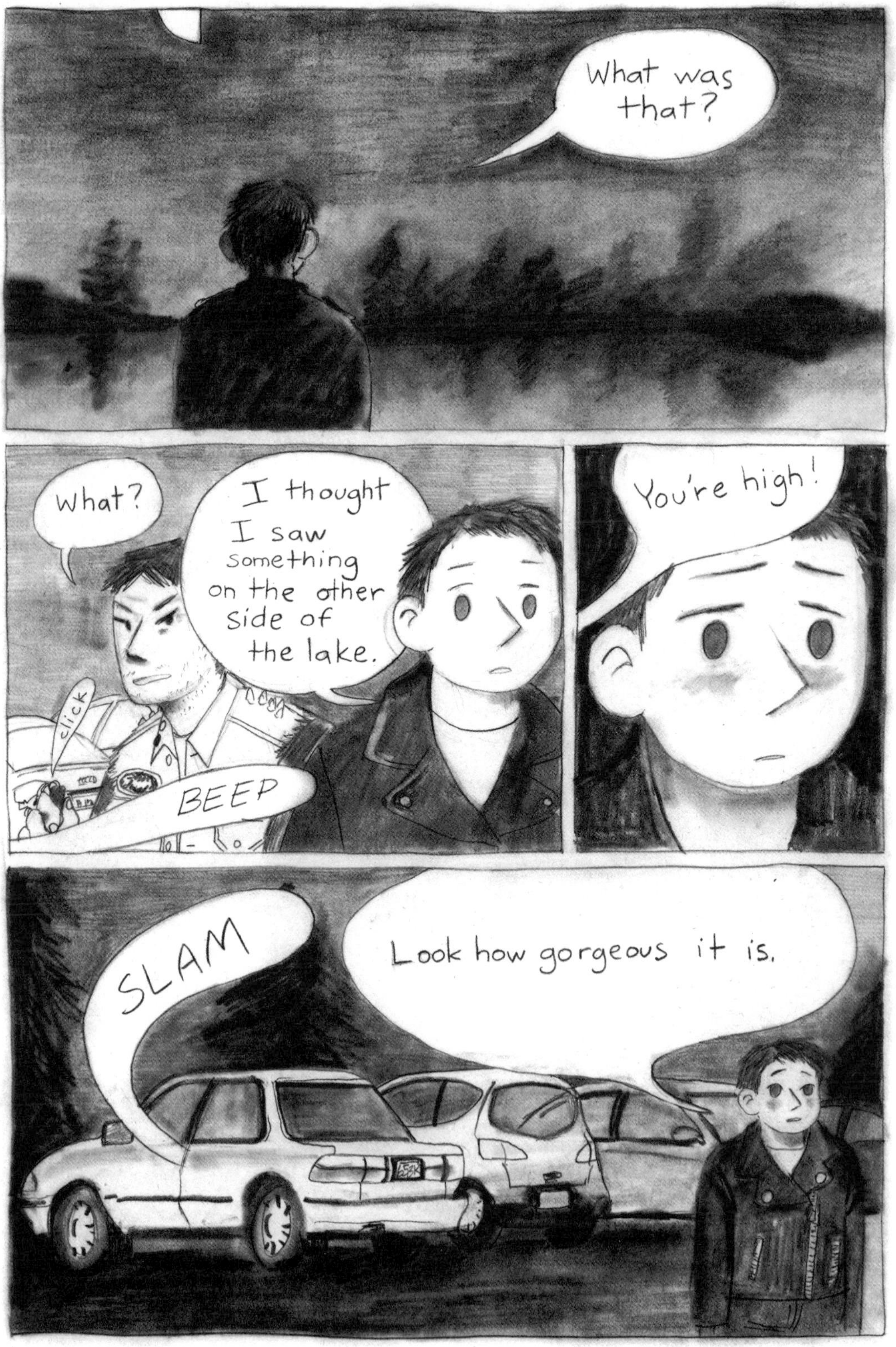
What was that?
What?
I thought I saw something on the other side of the lake.
click
BEEP
You're high!
SLAM
Look how gorgeous it is.

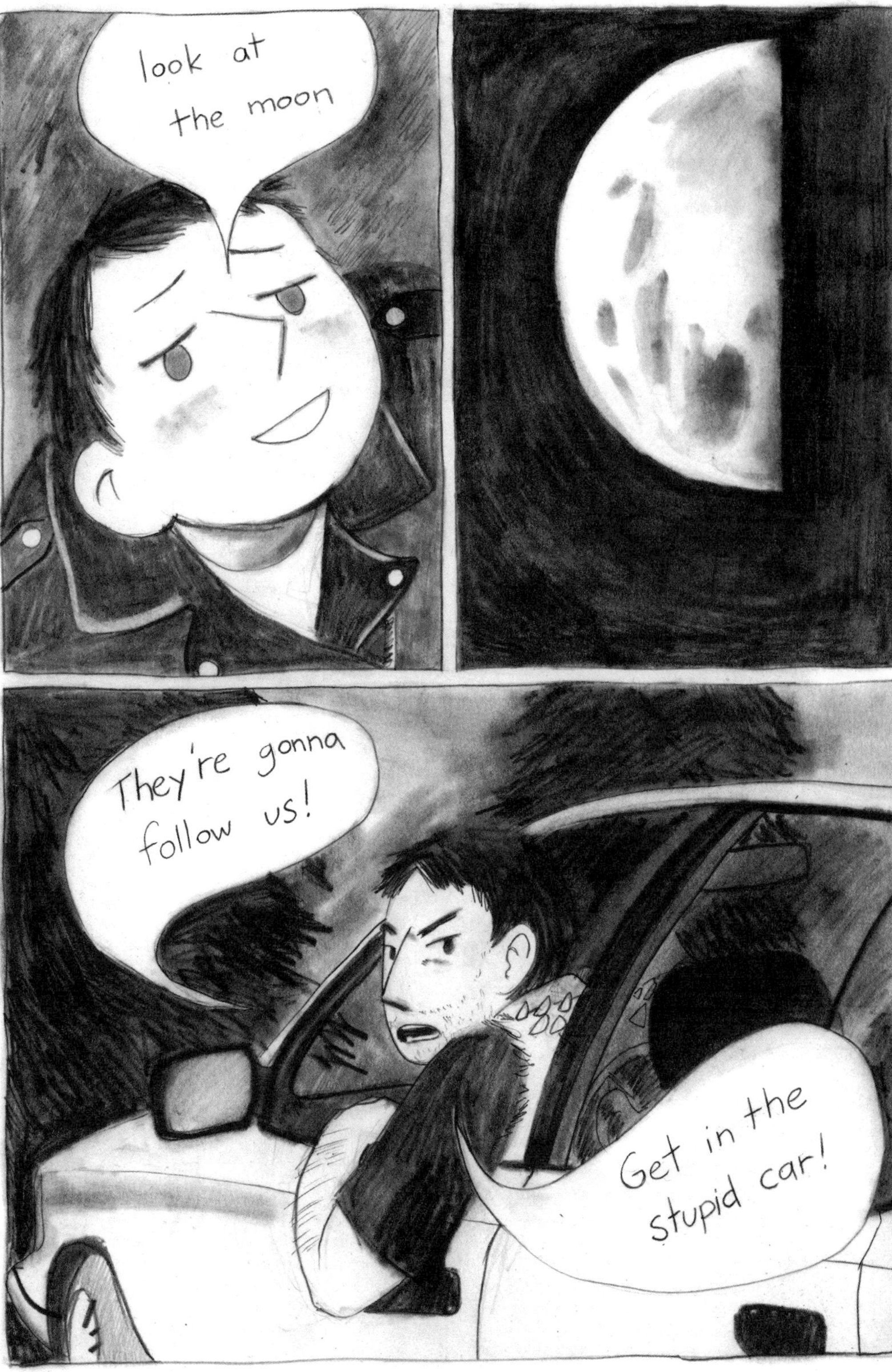
look at the moon
They're gonna follow us!
Get in the stupid car!

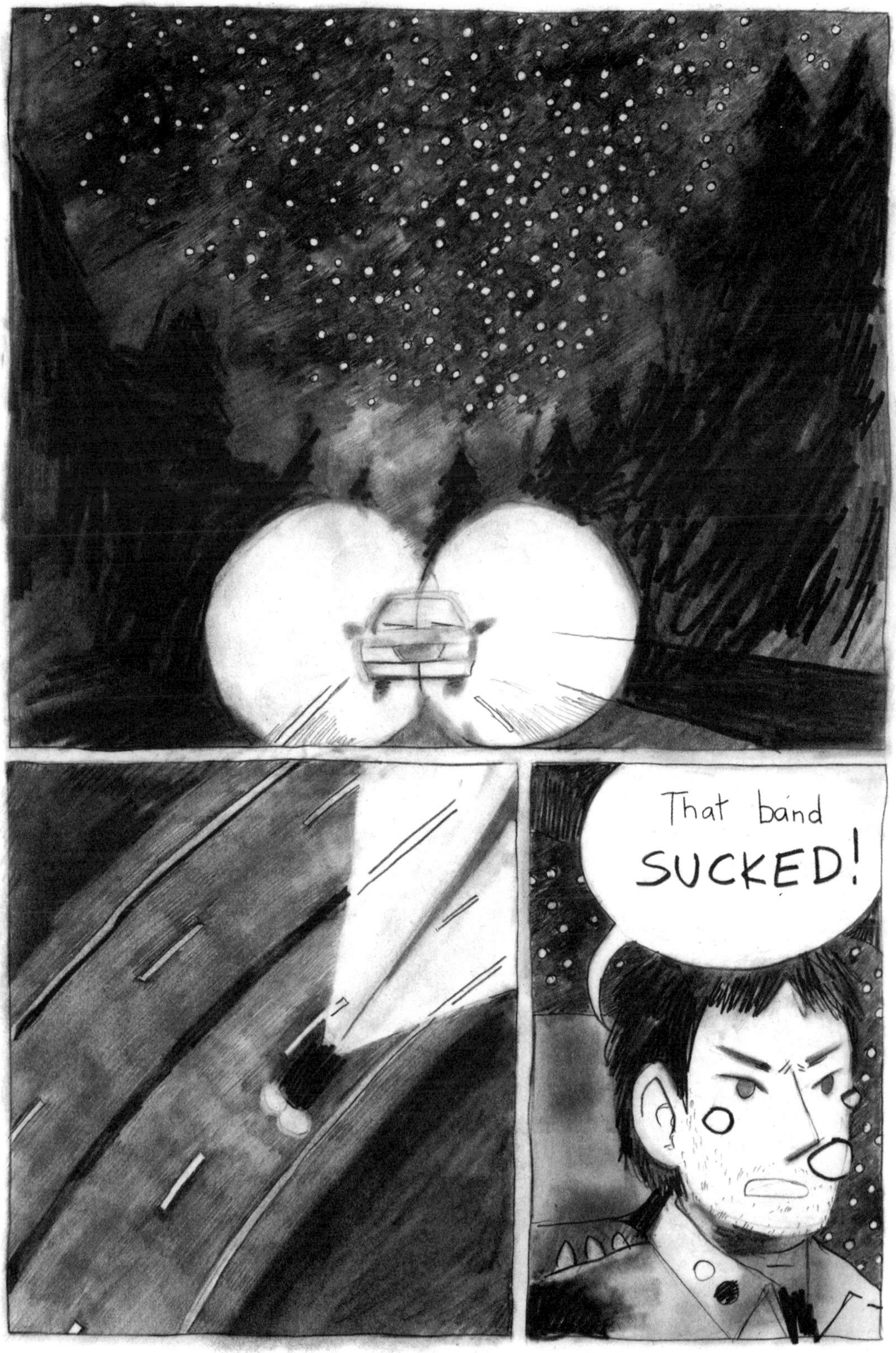
That band
SUCKED!

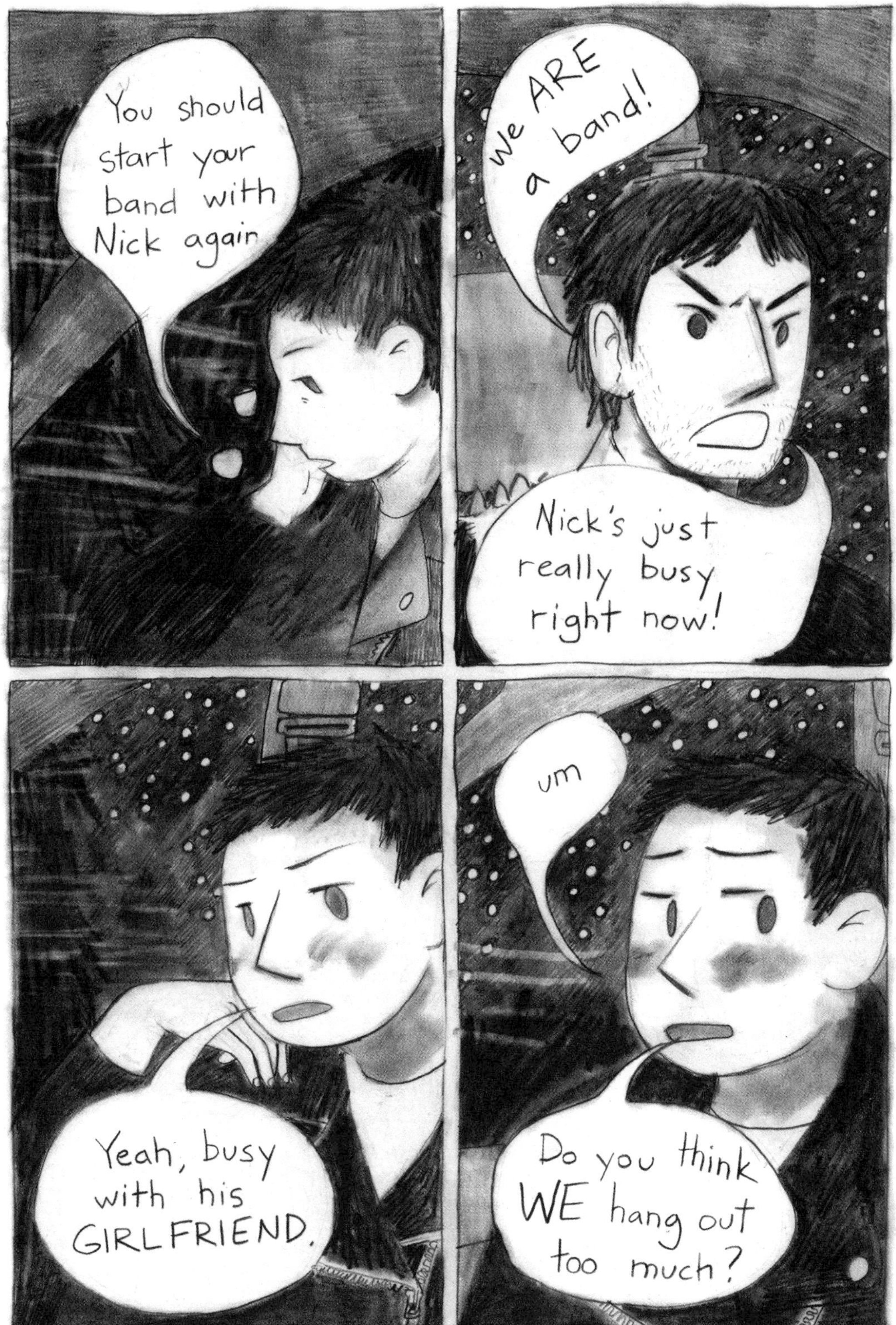
You should start your band with Nick again
We ARE a band!
Nick's just really busy right now!
Yeah, busy with his GIRLFRIEND.
um
Do you think WE hang out too much?

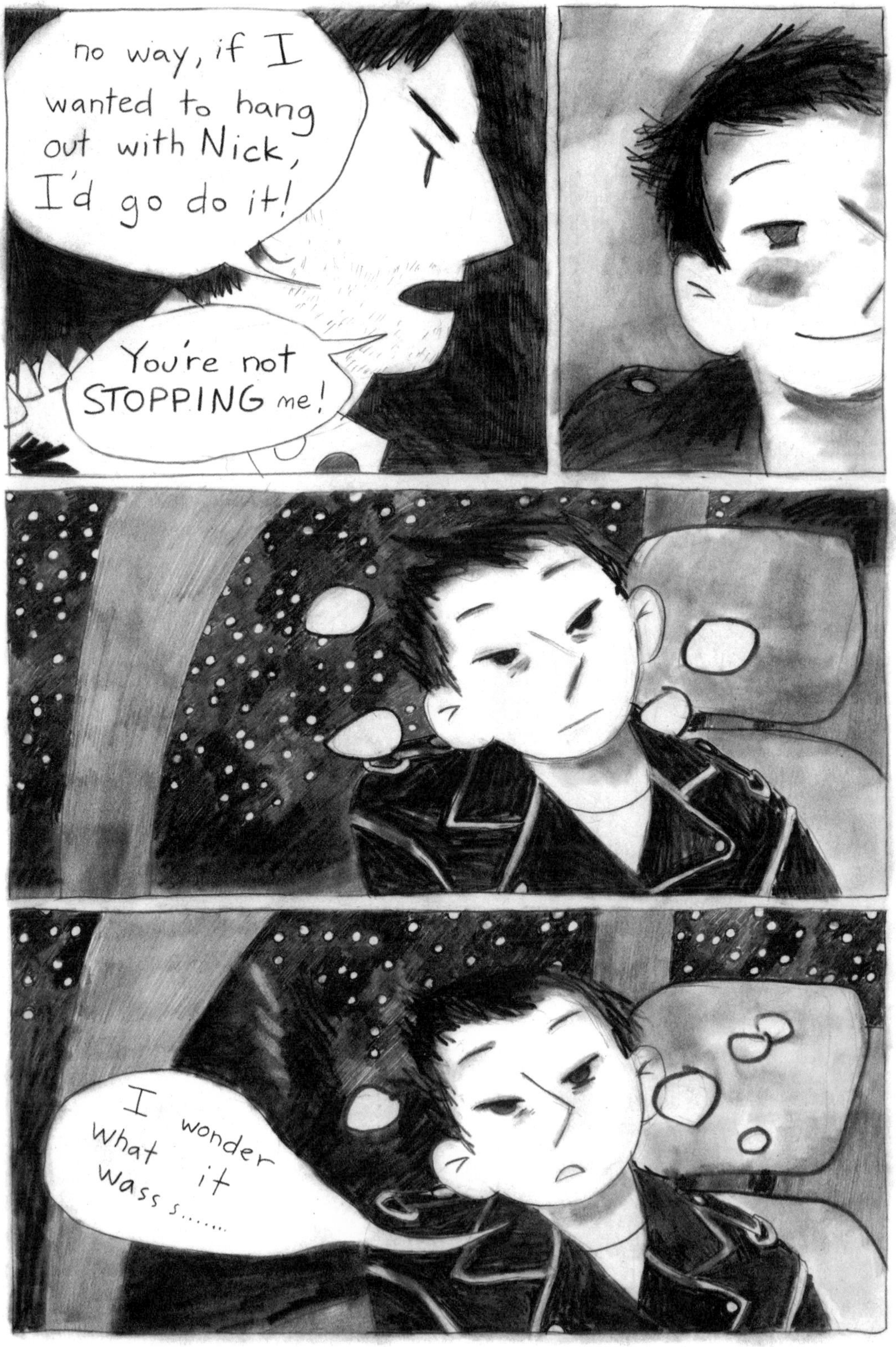
no way, if I wanted to hang out with Nick, I'd go do it!
You're not STOPPING me!
I wonder what it wasss......

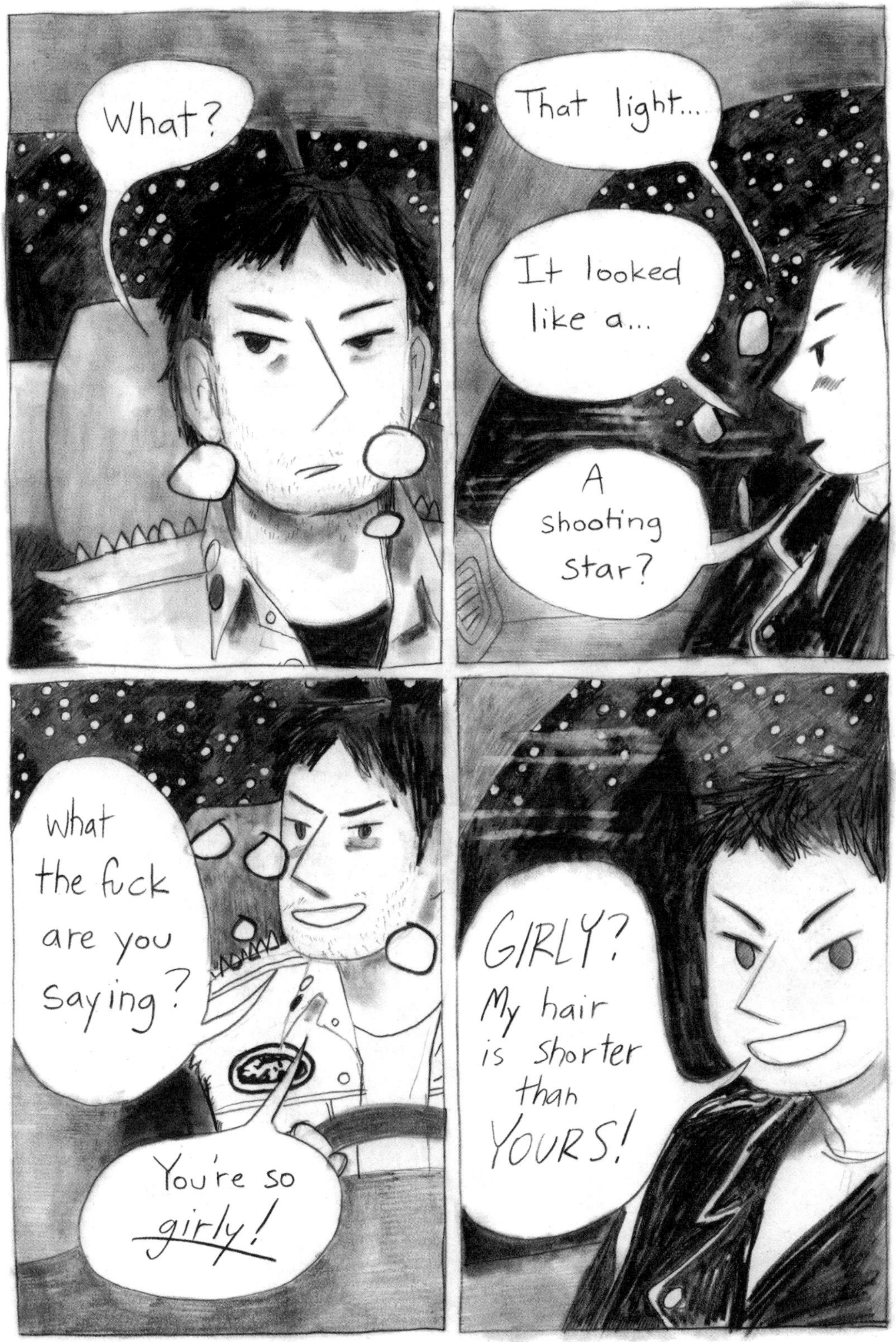
What?
That light...
It looked like a...
A shooting star?
What the fuck are you saying?
You're so girly!
GIRLY? My hair is shorter than YOURS!

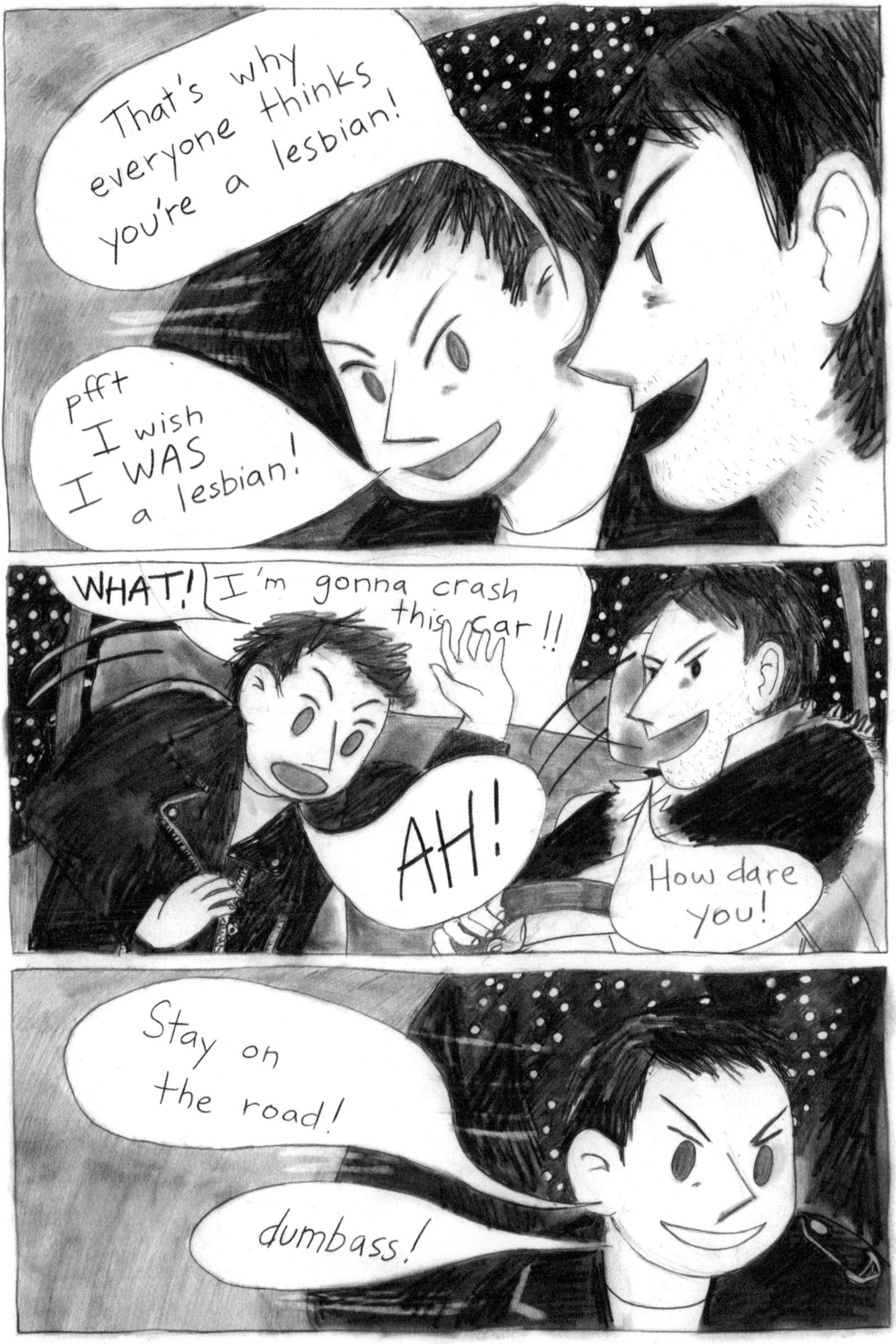
That's why everyone thinks you're a lesbian!
pfft I wish I WAS a lesbian!
WHAT!
I'm gonna crash this car!!
AH!
How dare you!
Stay on the road!
dumbass!

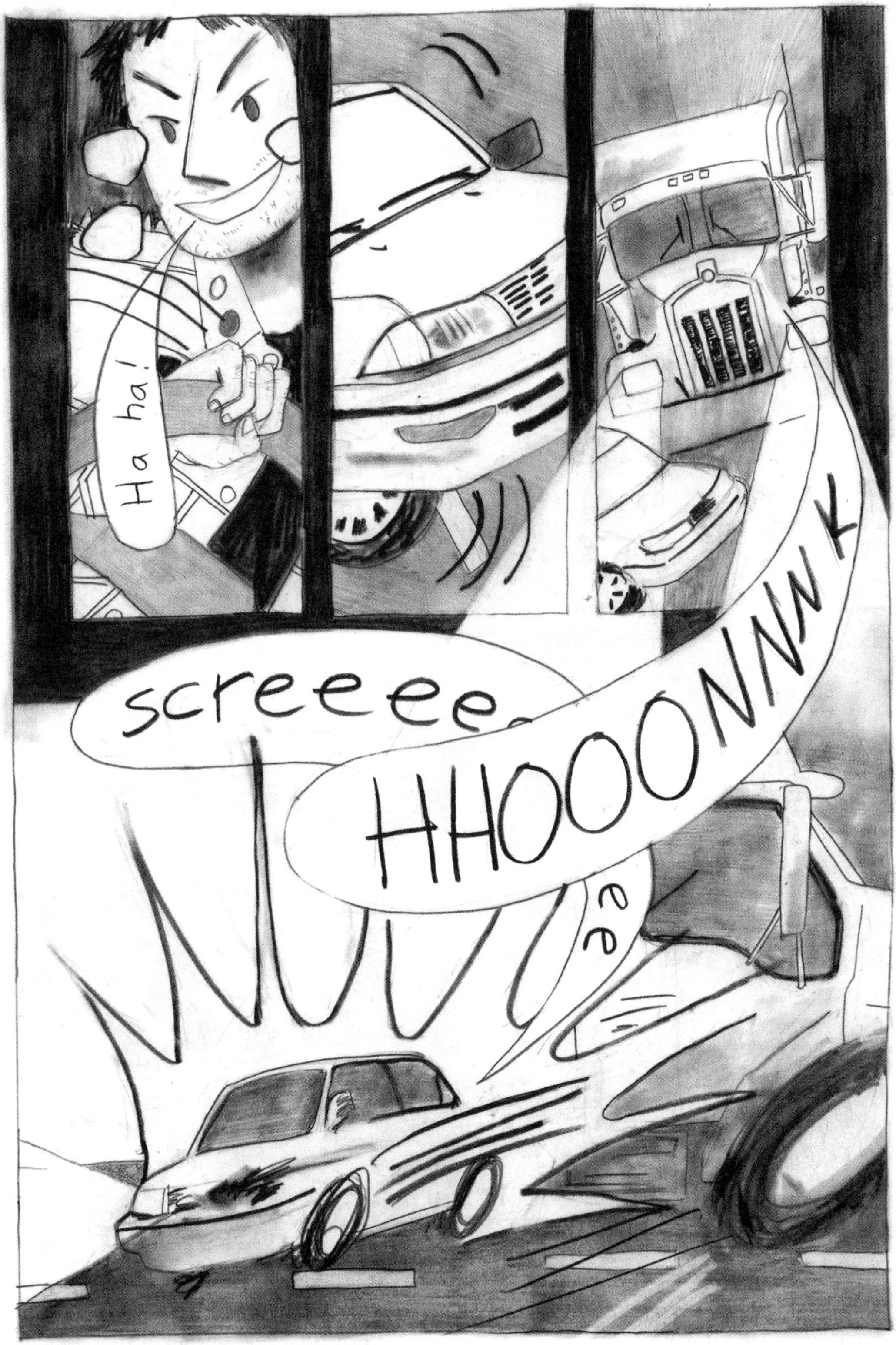
Ha ha!
screeeeee
HHOOONNWK

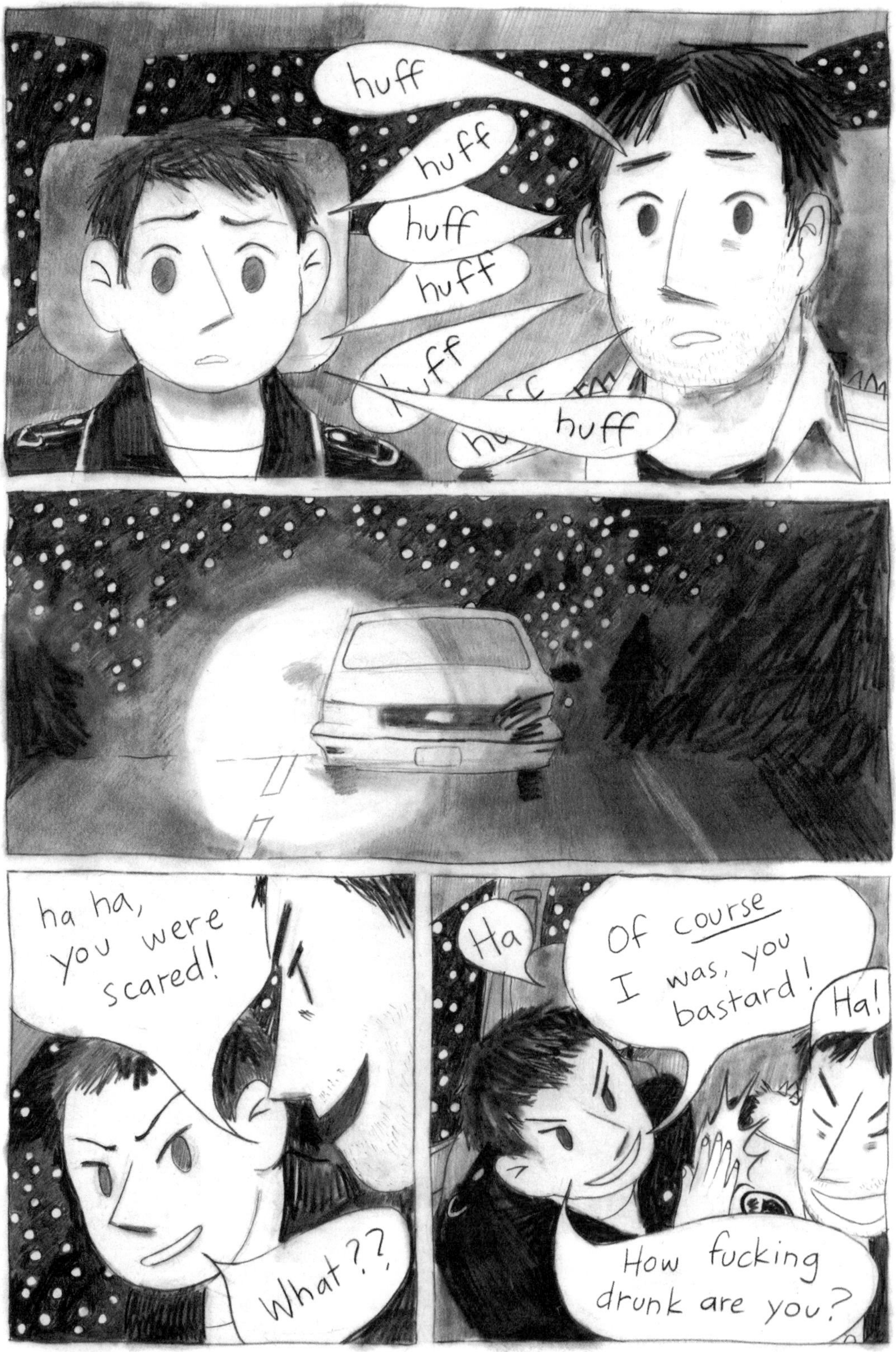
huff
huff
huff
huff
huff
huff
ha ha, you were scared!
What??
Ha
Of course I was, you bastard!
Ha!
How fucking drunk are you?

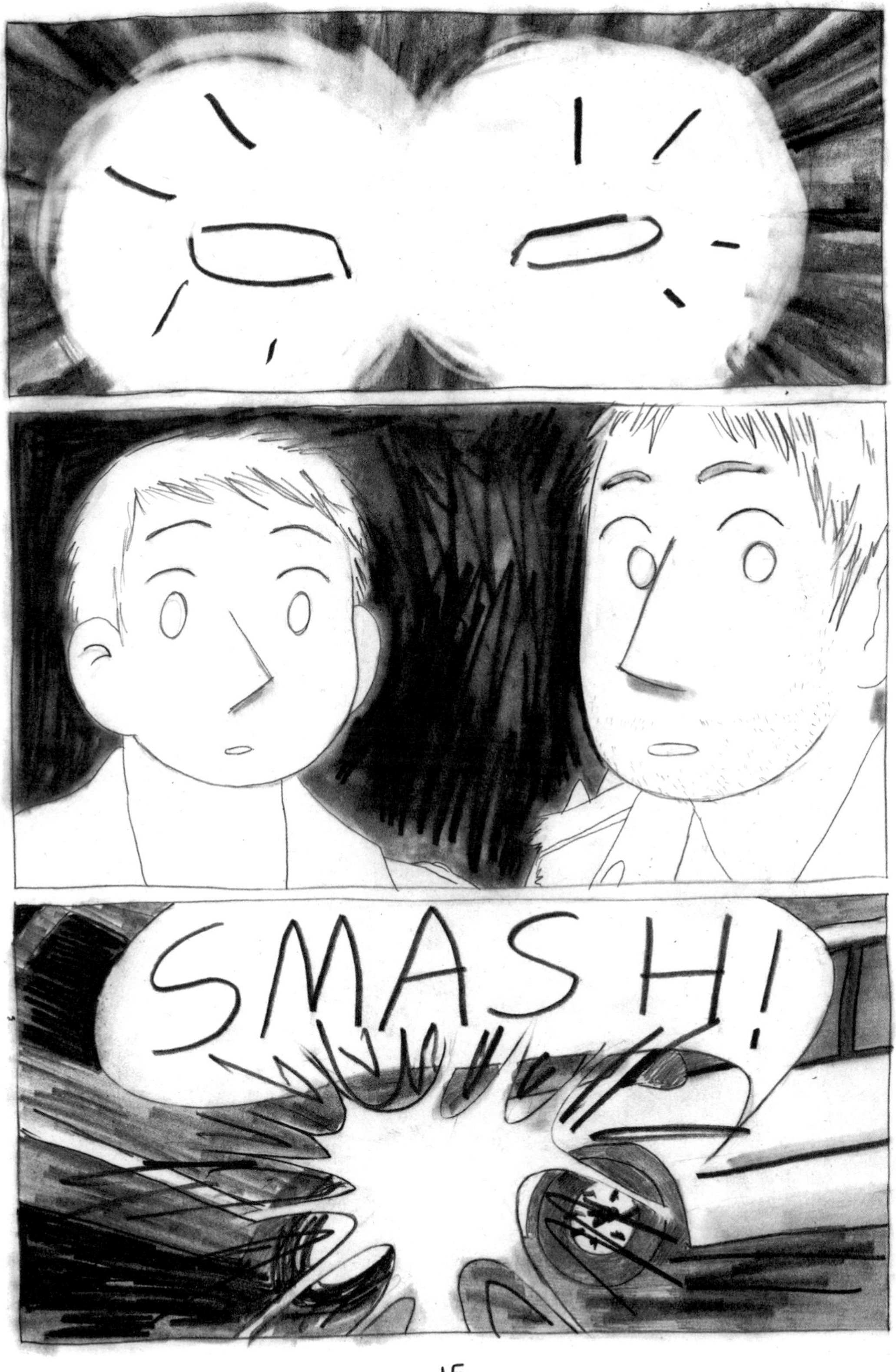
SMASH!

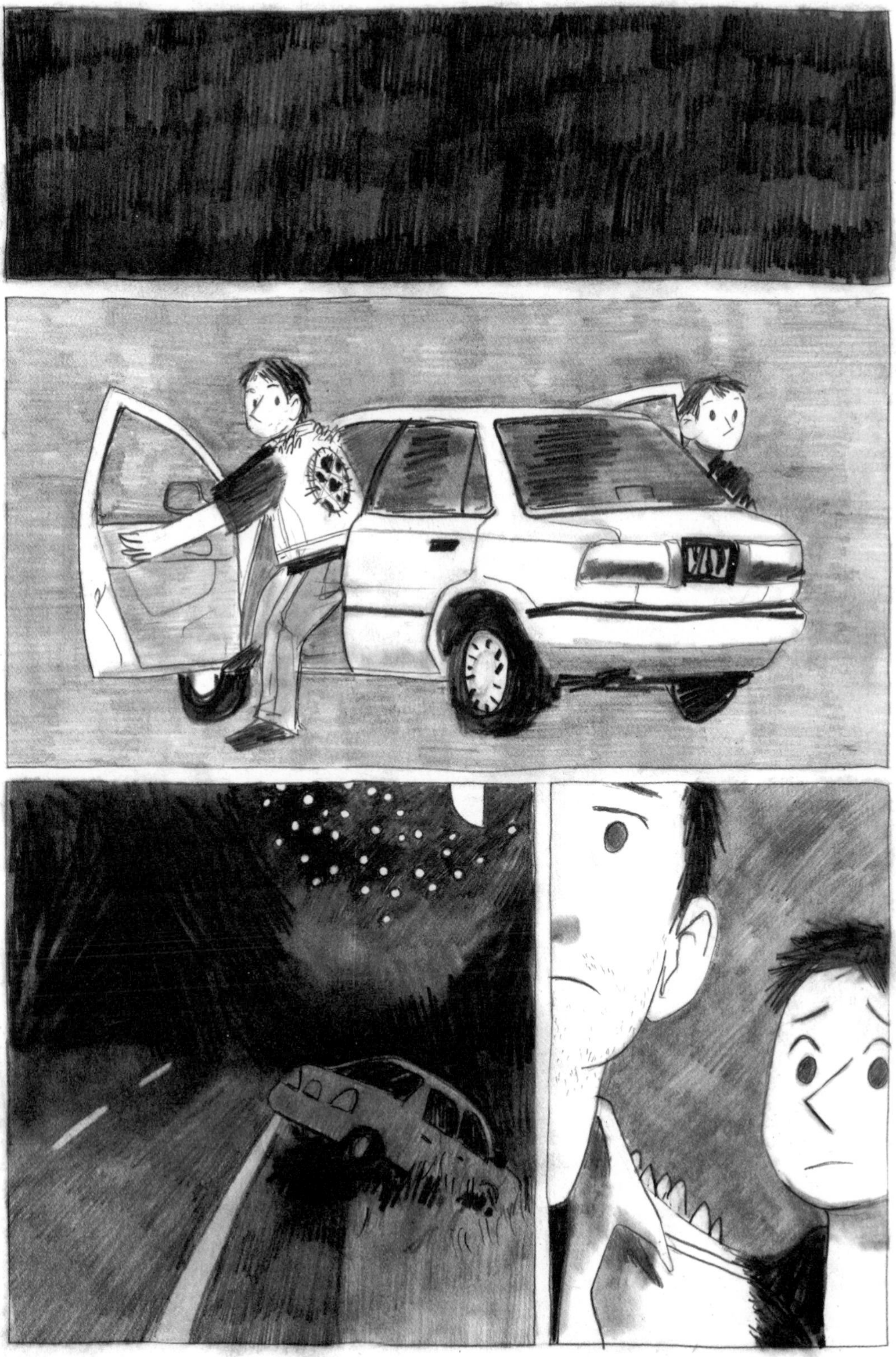

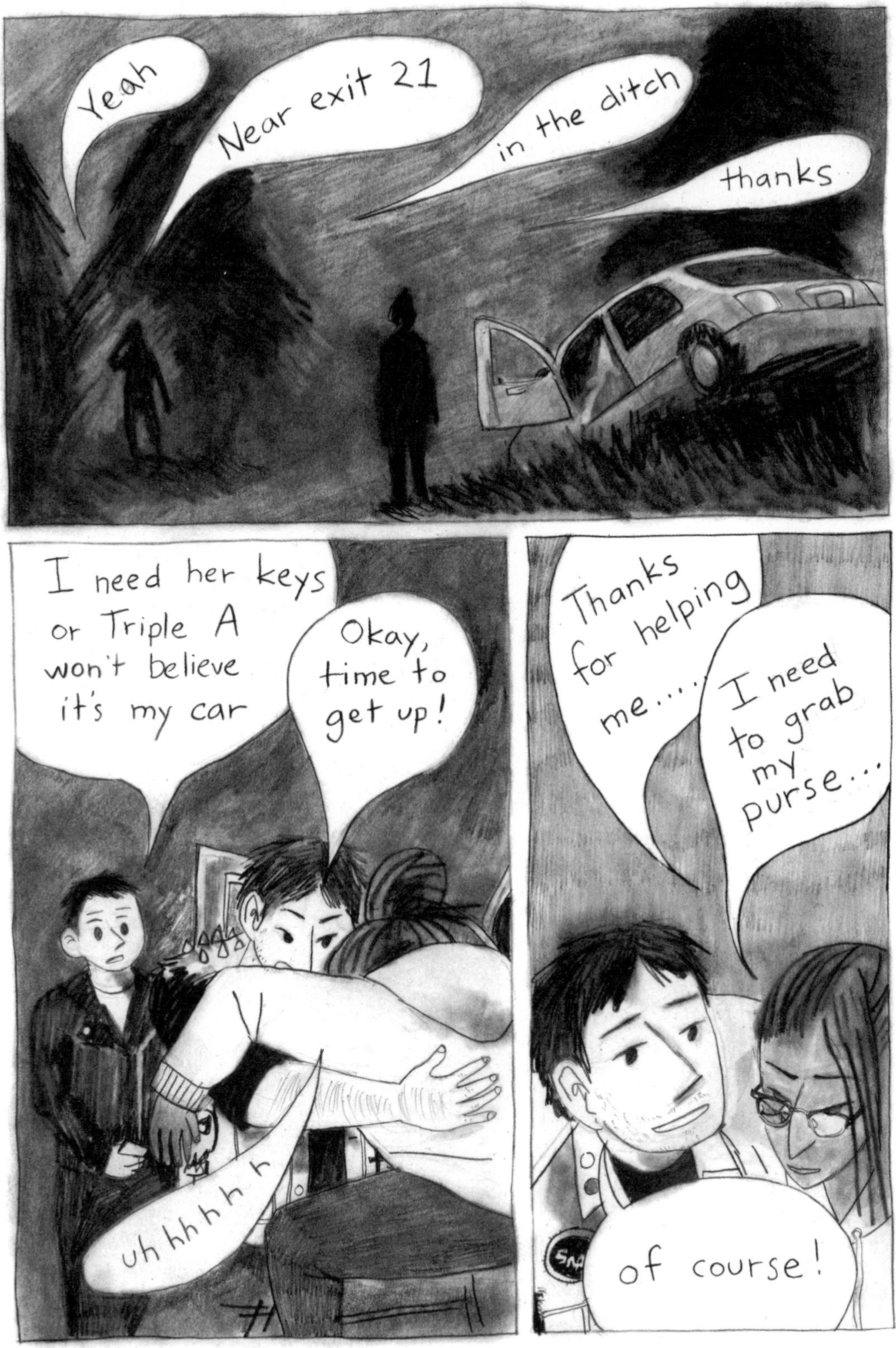
Yeah
Near exit 21
in the ditch
thanks
I need her keys or Triple A won't believe it's my car
Okay, time to get up!
uhhhhh
Thanks for helping me.....
I need to grab my purse...
of course!

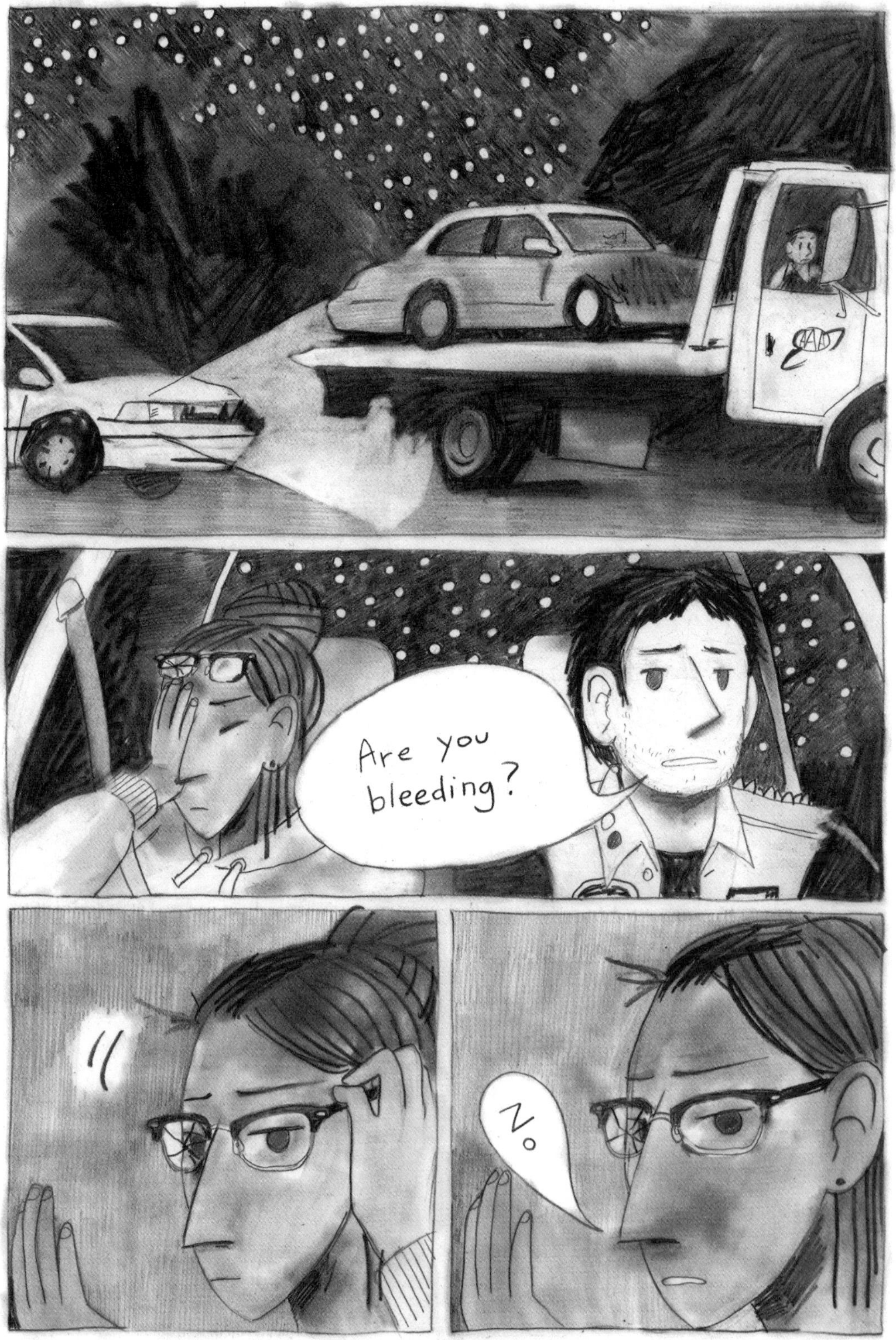
Are you bleeding?
No

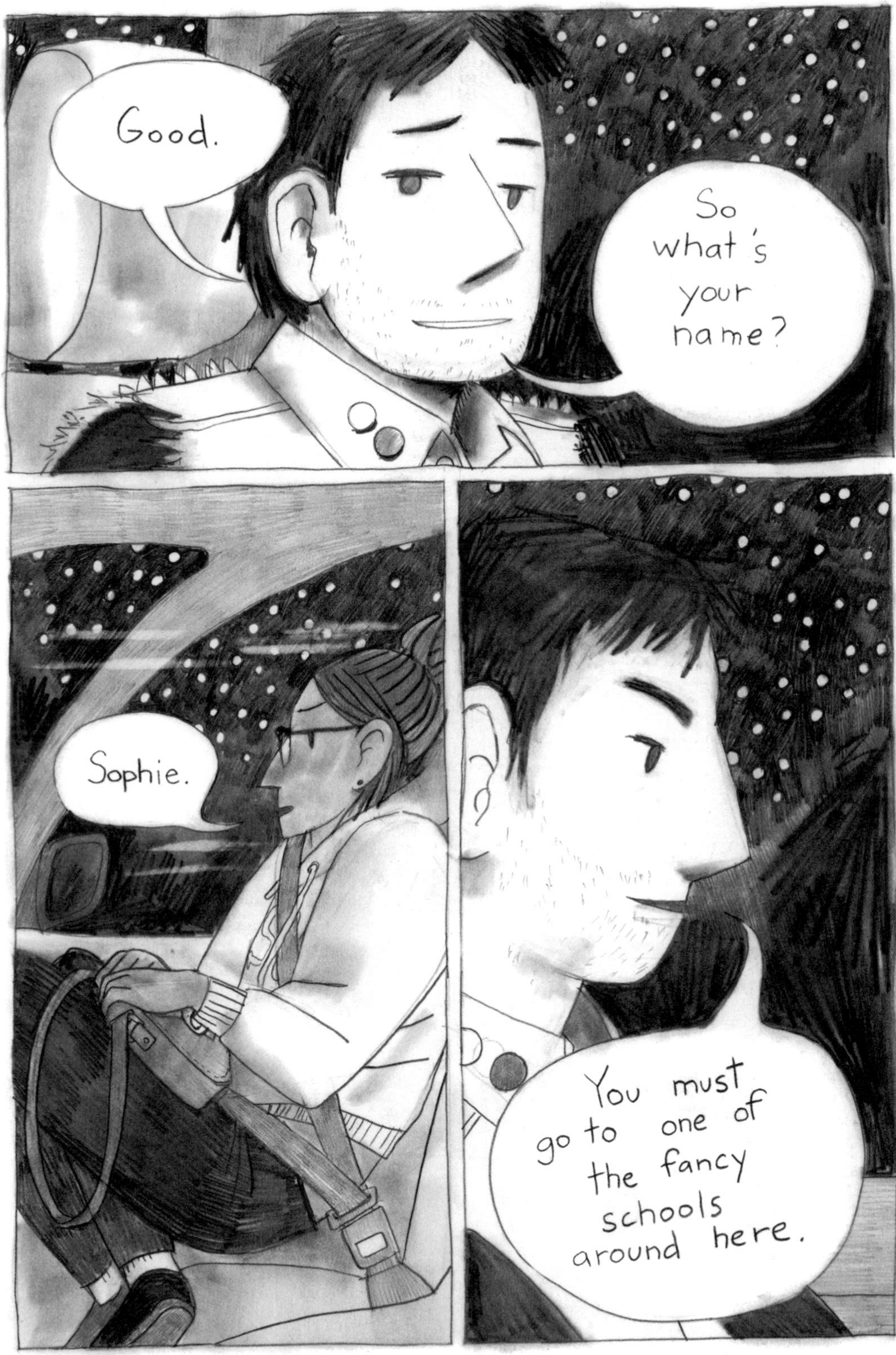
Good.
So what's your name?
Sophie.
You must go to one of the fancy schools around here.

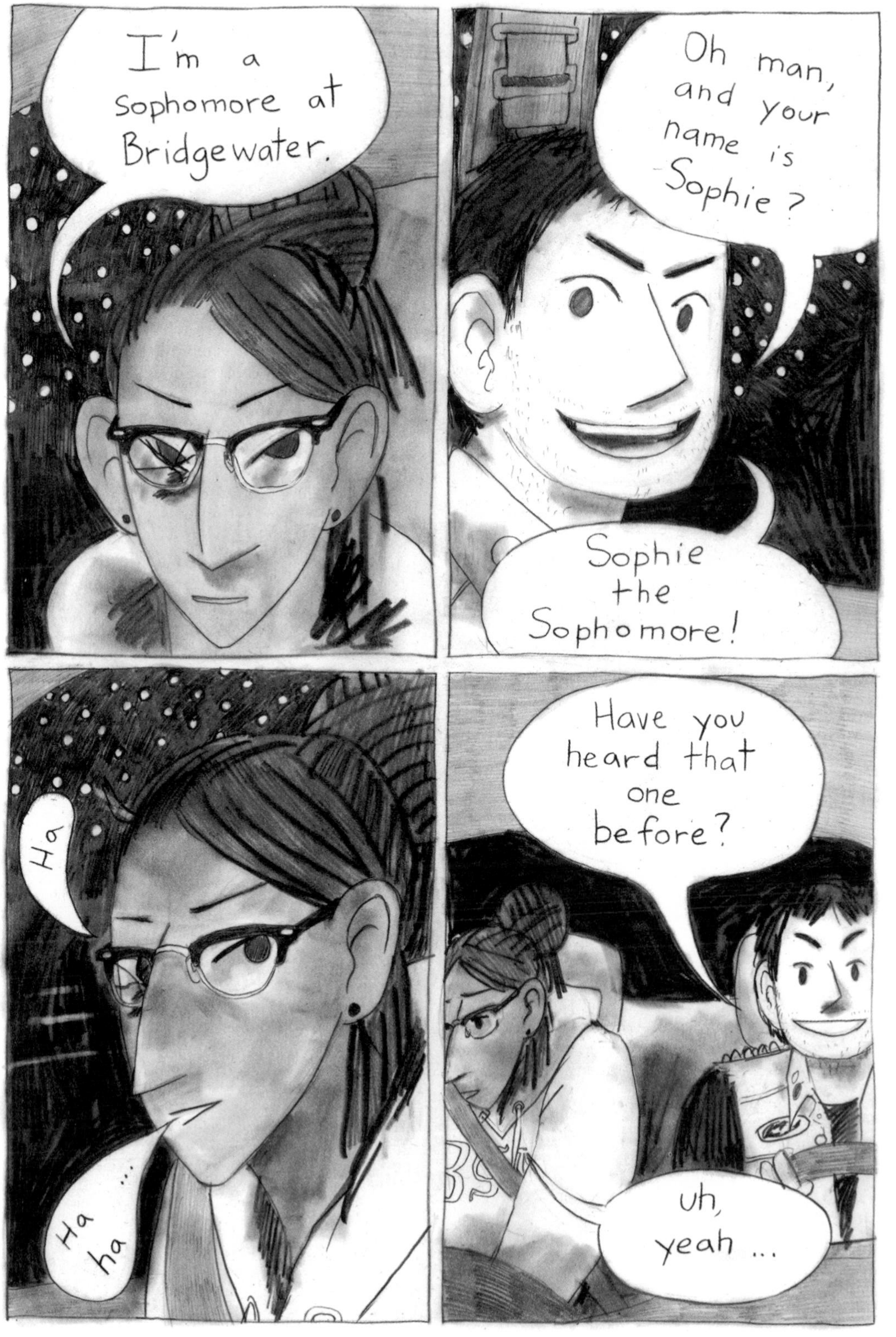
I'm a sophomore at Bridgewater.
Oh man, and your name is Sophie?
Sophie the Sophomore!
Ha
Ha ha ...
Have you heard that one before?
uh, yeah ...

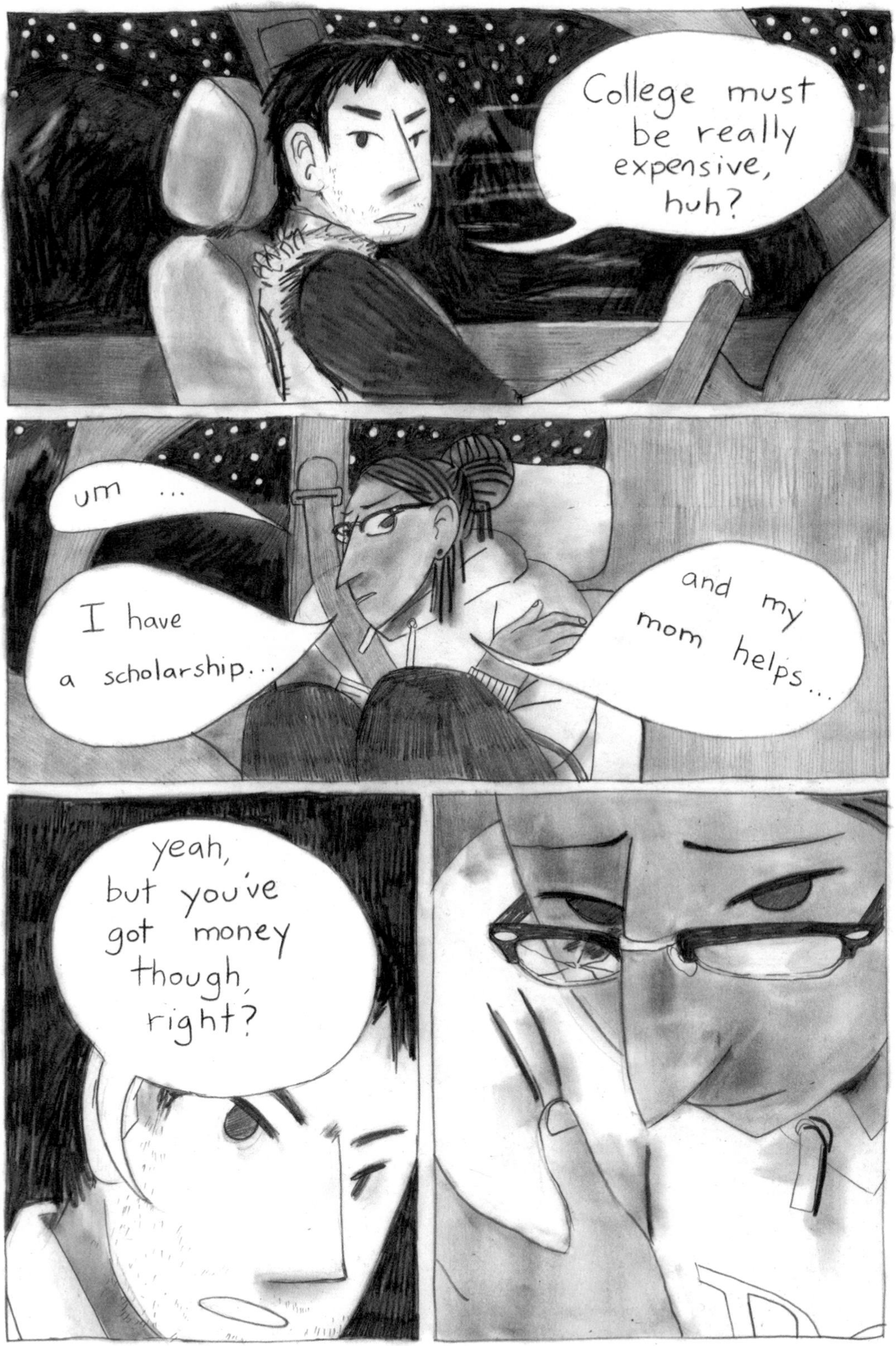
College must be really expensive, huh?
um ...
I have a scholarship...
and my mom helps...
yeah, but you've got money though, right?

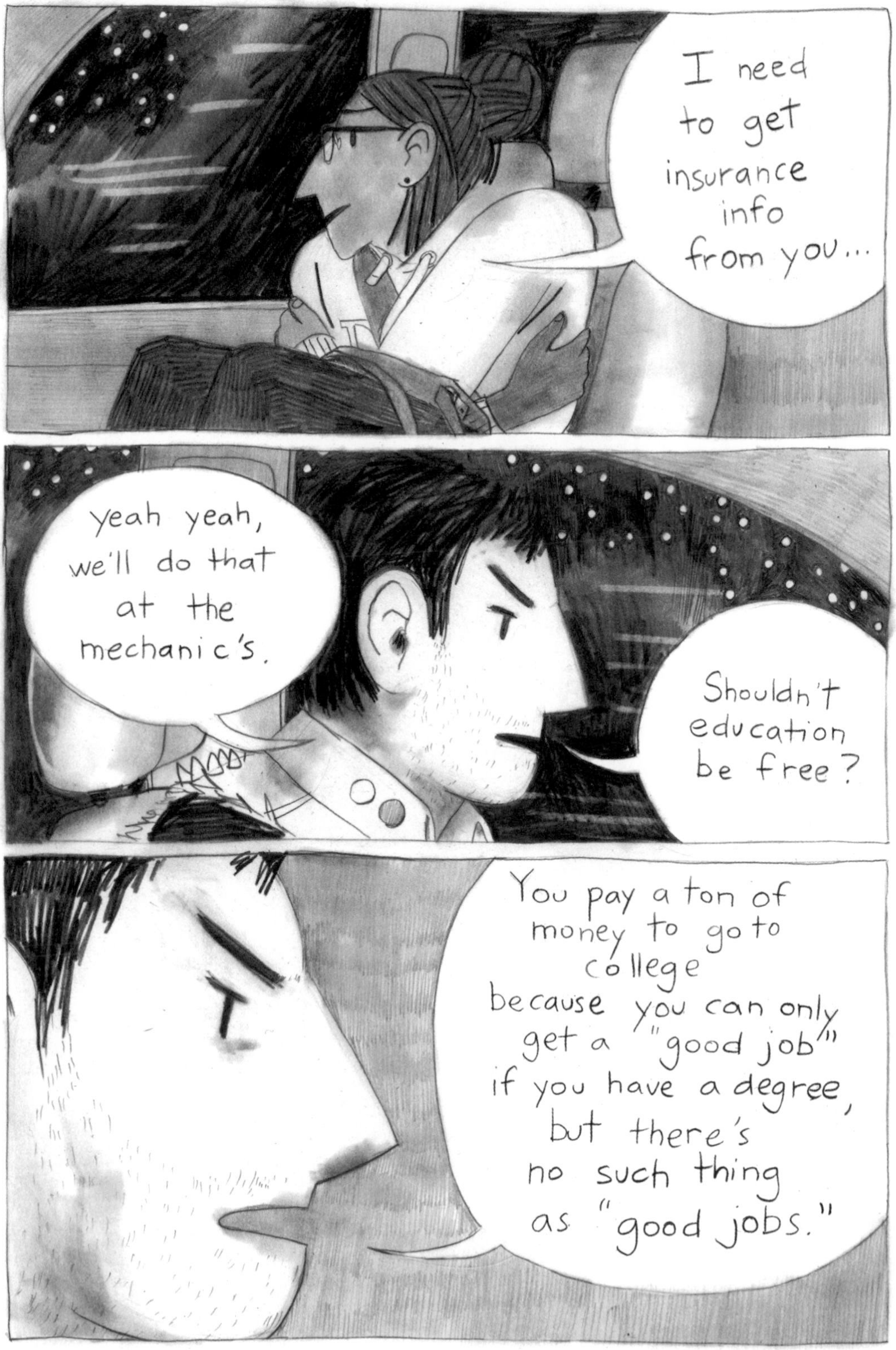
I need to get insurance info from you...
yeah yeah, we'll do that at the mechanic's.
Shouldn't education be free?
You pay a ton of money to go to college because you can only get a "good job" if you have a degree, but there's no such thing as "good jobs."

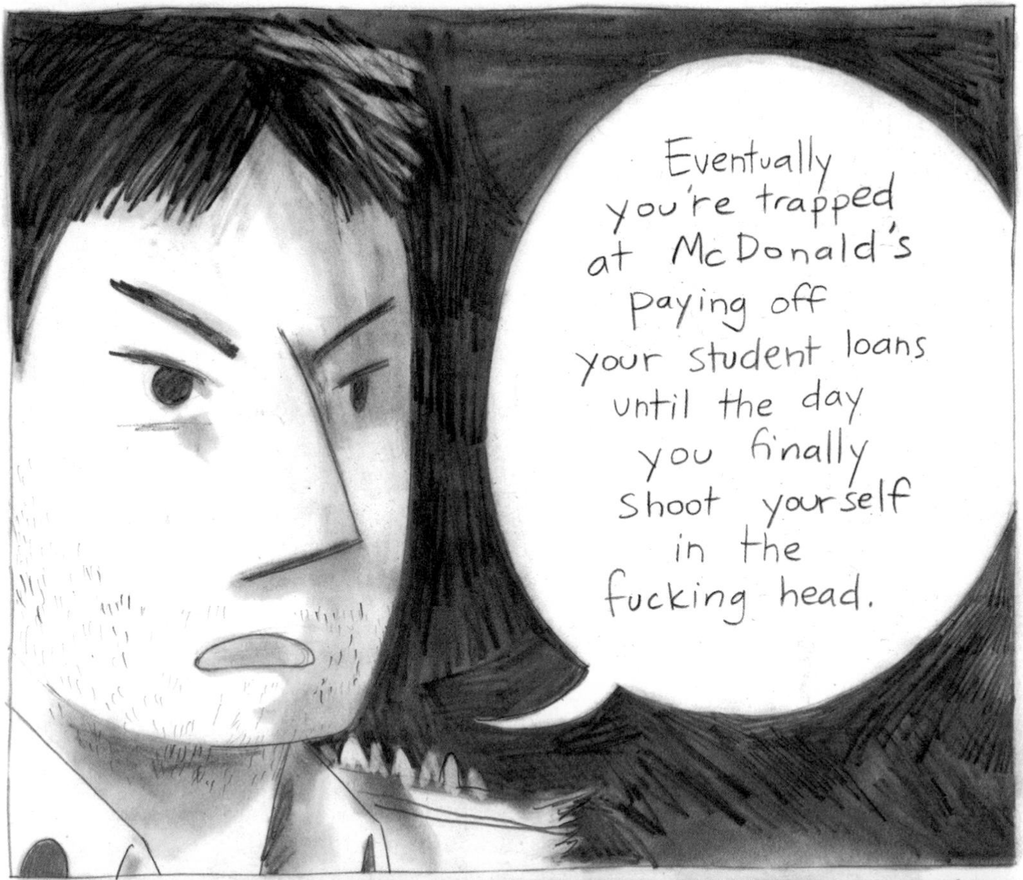
Eventually you're trapped at McDonald's paying off your student loans until the day you finally shoot yourself in the fucking head.

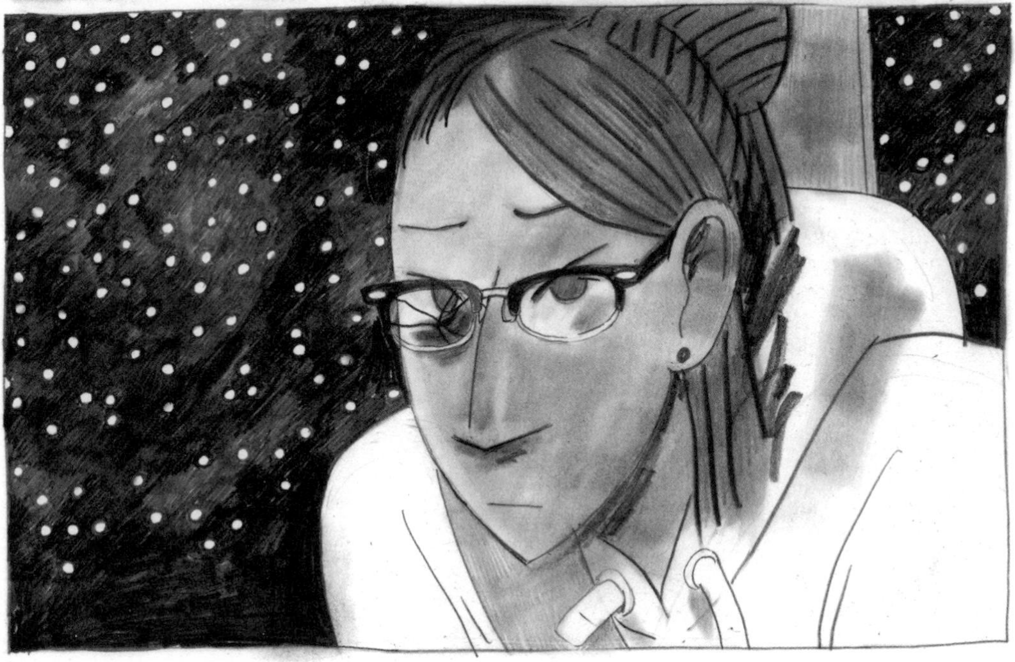

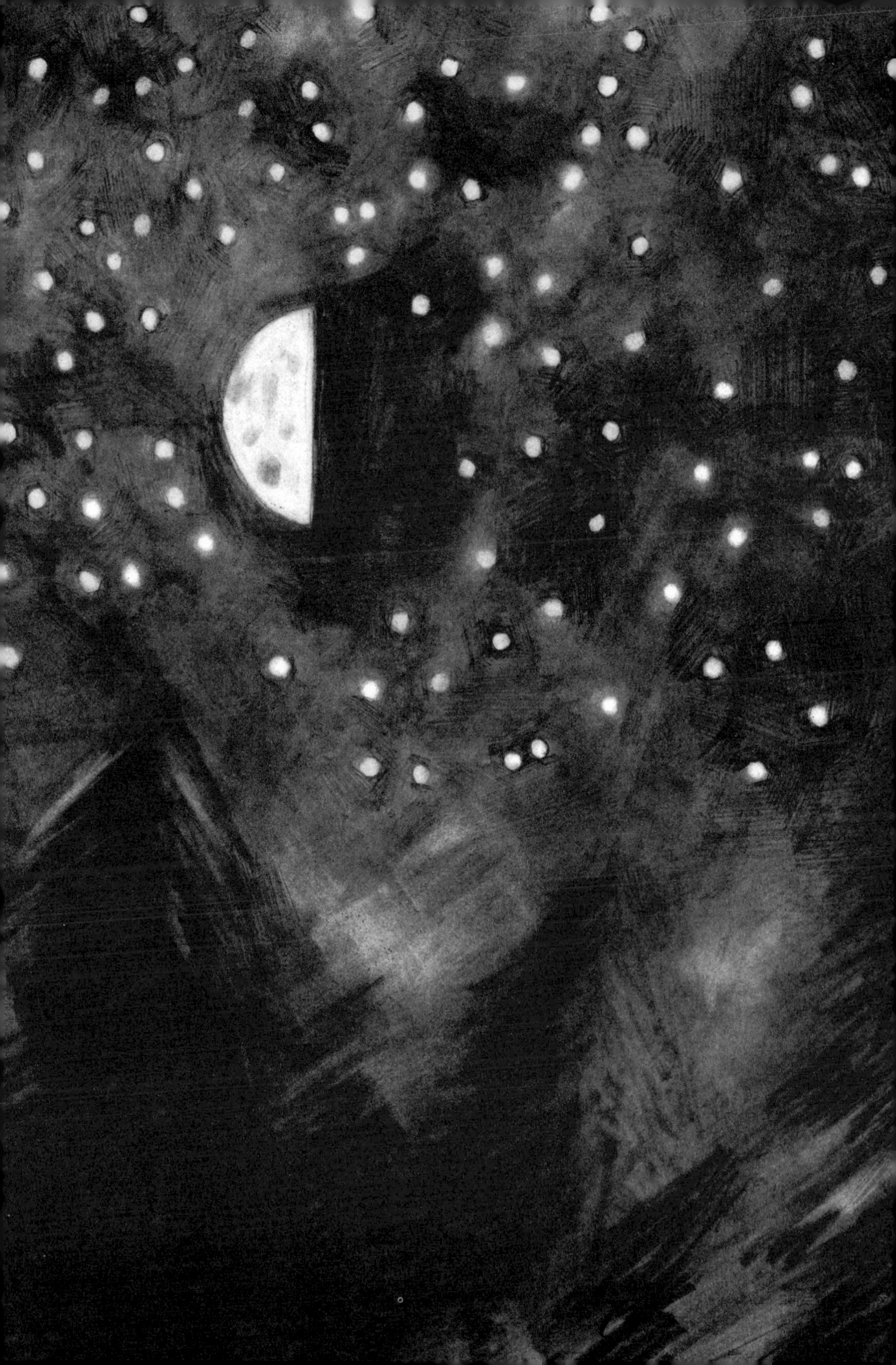

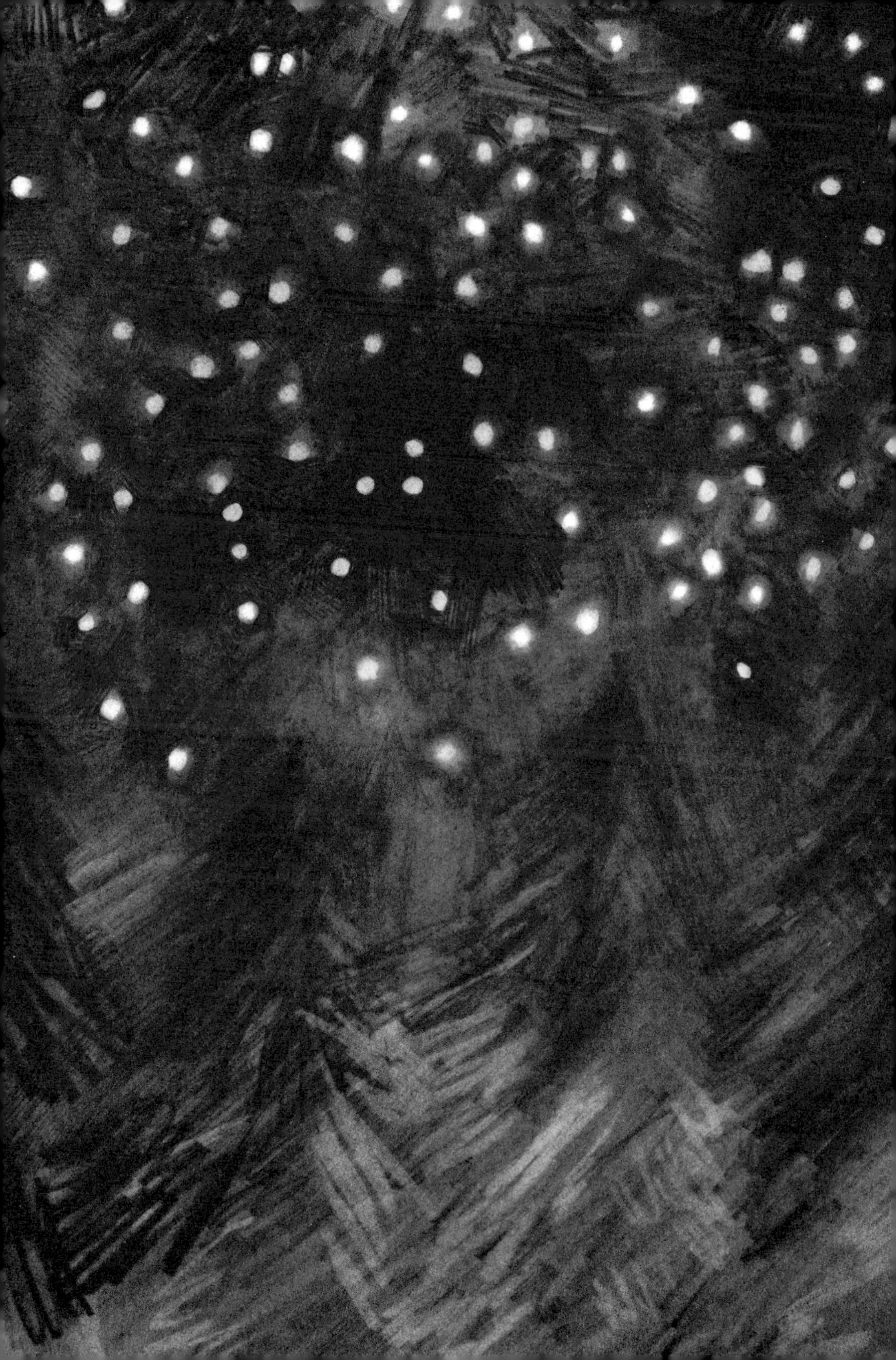

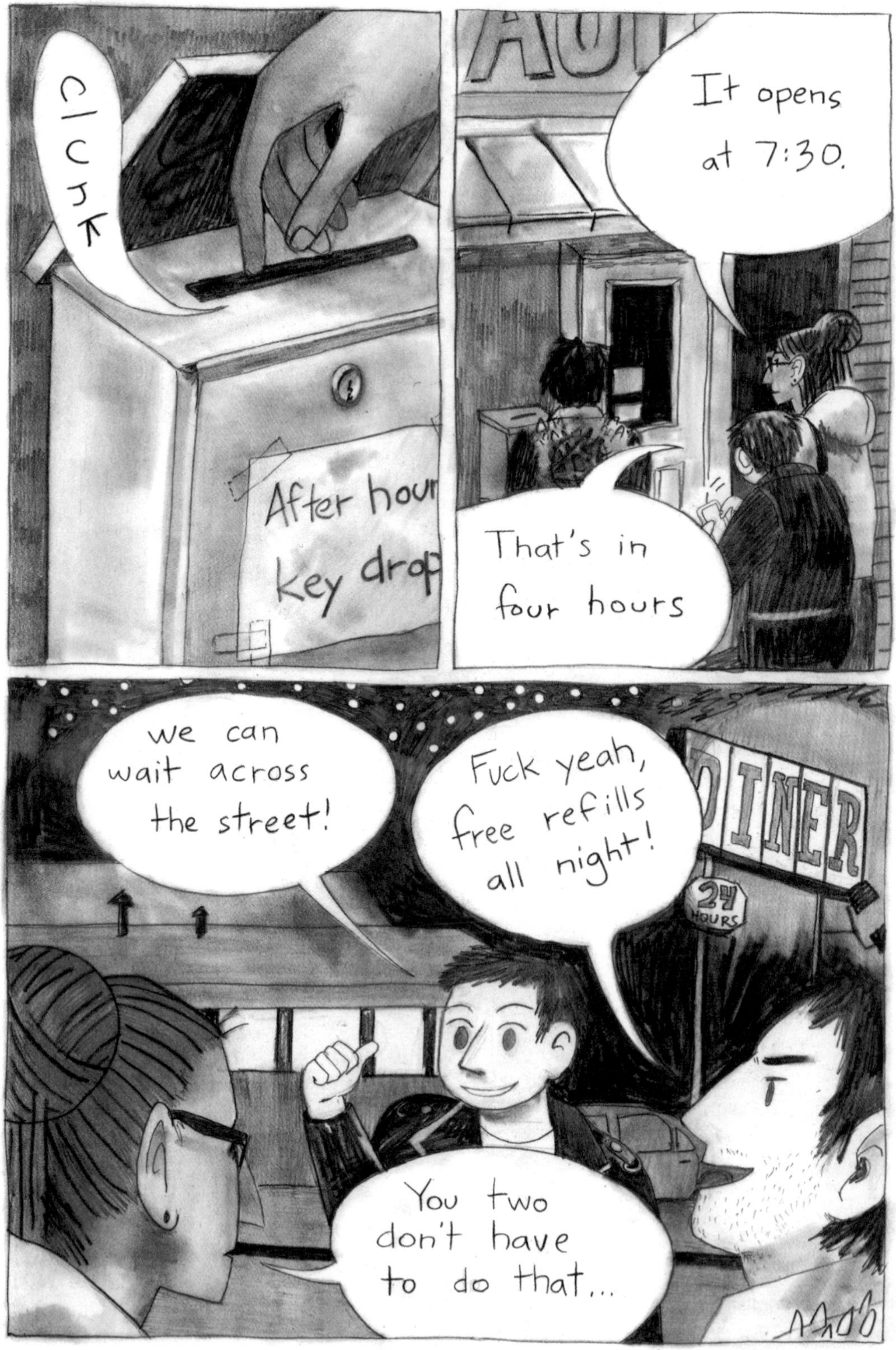
CLUNK
After hour
key drop
It opens at 7:30.
That's in four hours
we can wait across the street!
Fuck yeah, free refills all night!
DINER
24 HOURS
You two don't have to do that...

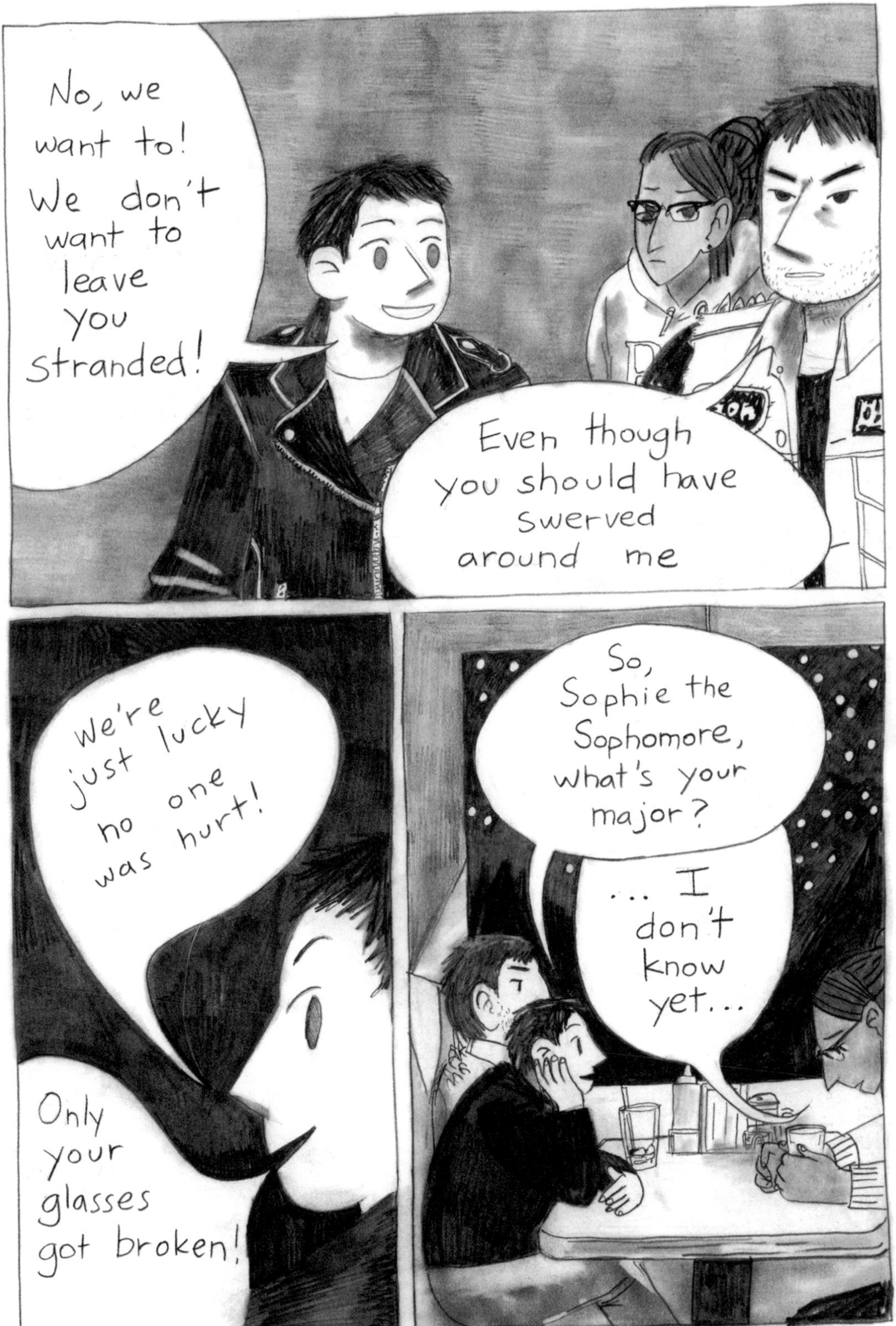
No, we want to! We don't want to leave you stranded!
Even though you should have swerved around me
We're just lucky no one was hurt!
Only your glasses got broken!
So, Sophie the Sophomore, what's your major?
... I don't know yet...

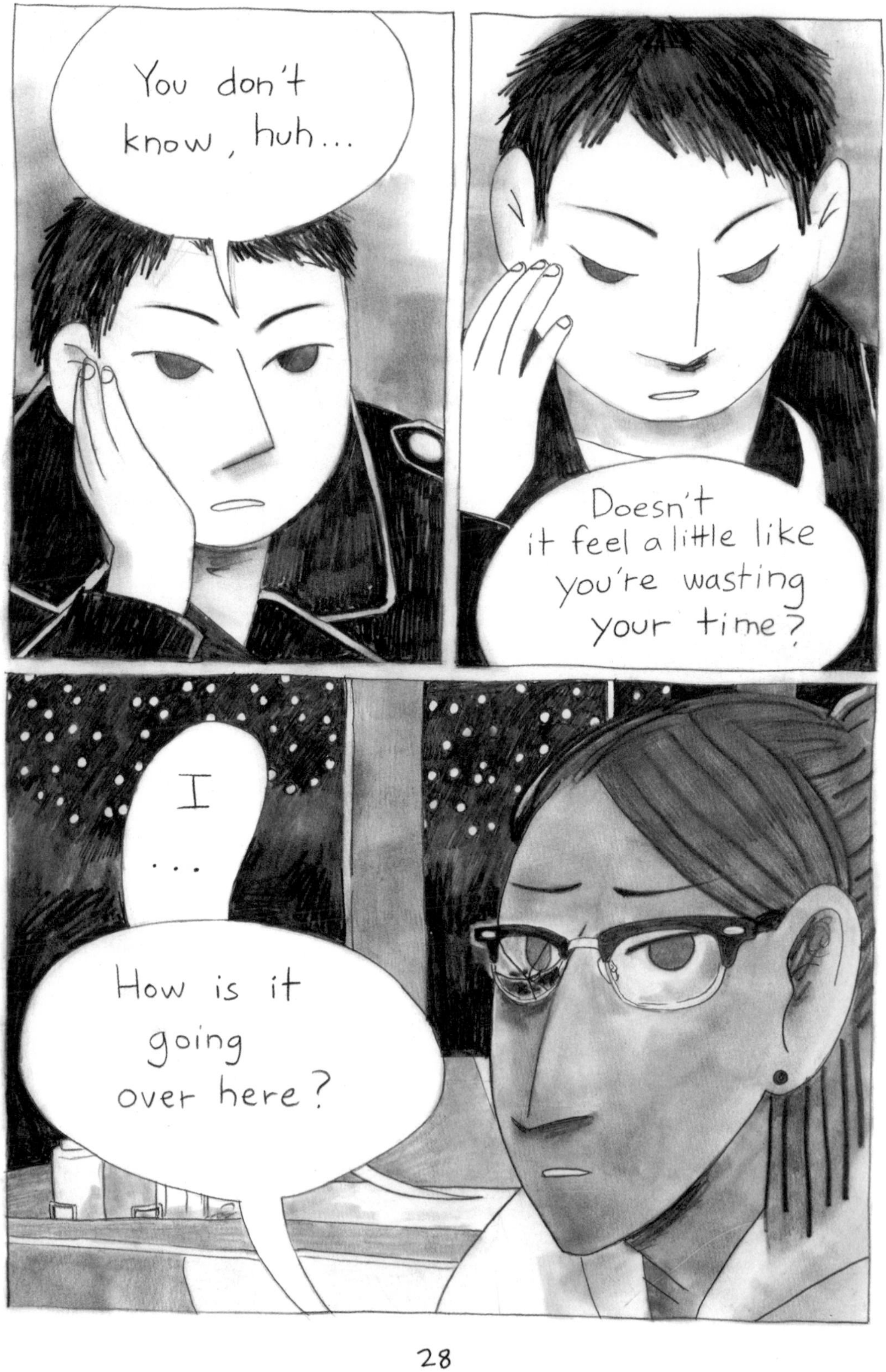
You don't know, huh...
Doesn't it feel a little like you're wasting your time?
I ...
How is it going over here?

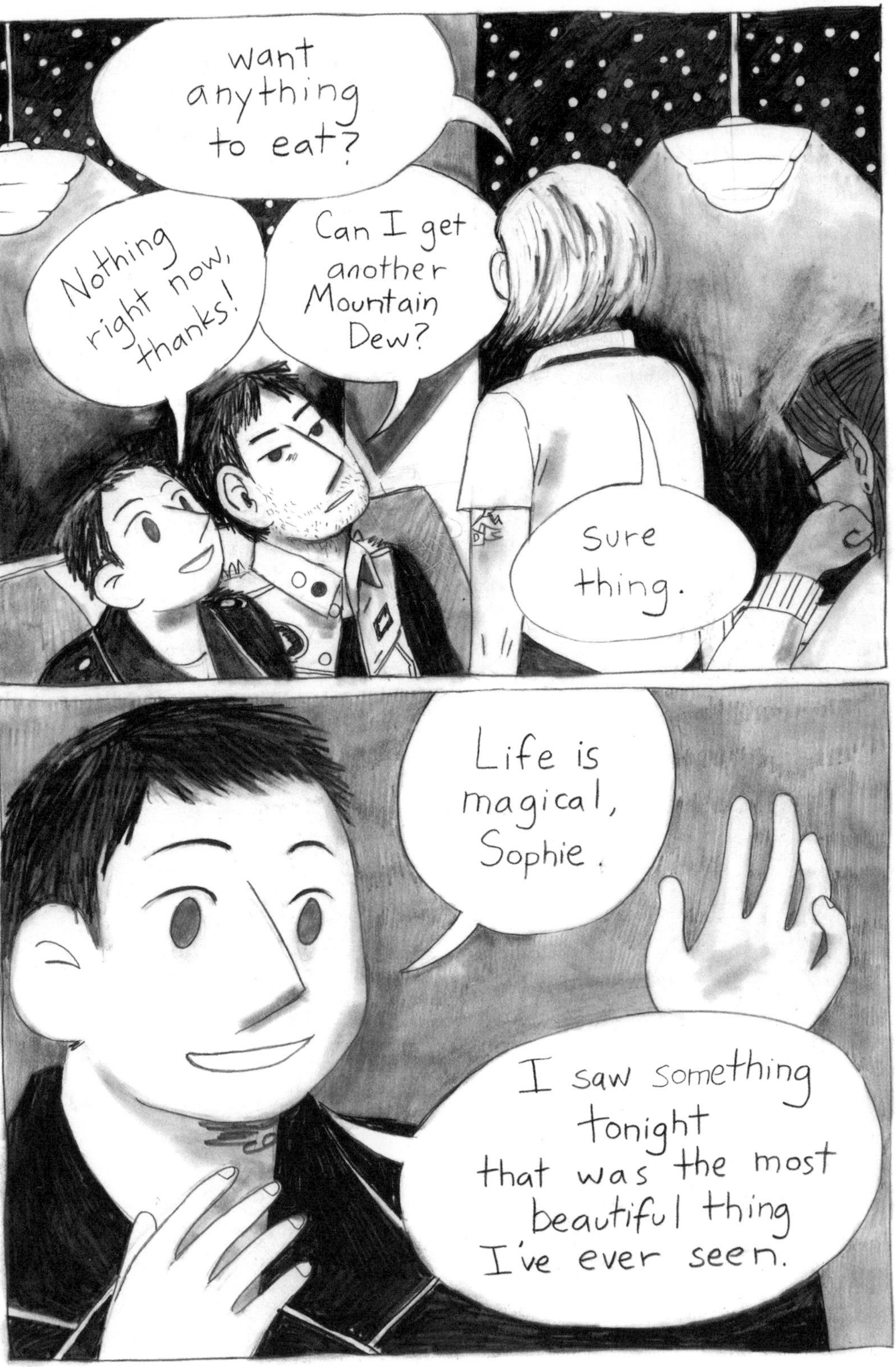
want anything to eat?
Nothing right now, thanks!
Can I get another Mountain Dew?
Sure thing.
Life is magical, Sophie.
I saw something tonight that was the most beautiful thing I've ever seen.

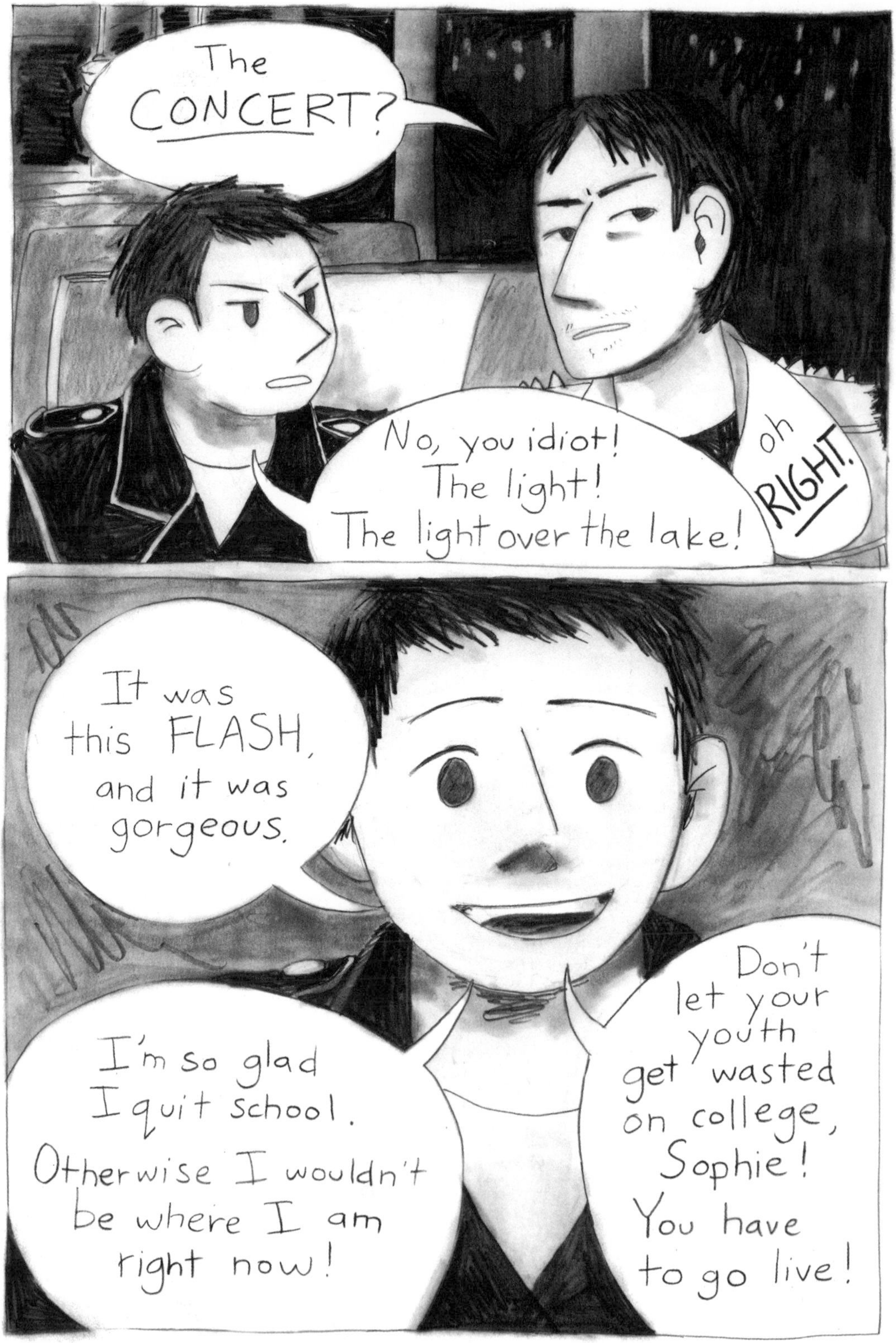

The CONCERT?
No, you idiot! The light! The light over the lake!
oh RIGHT.
It was this FLASH, and it was gorgeous.
I'm so glad I quit school. Otherwise I wouldn't be where I am right now!
Don't let your youth get wasted on college, Sophie! You have to go live!

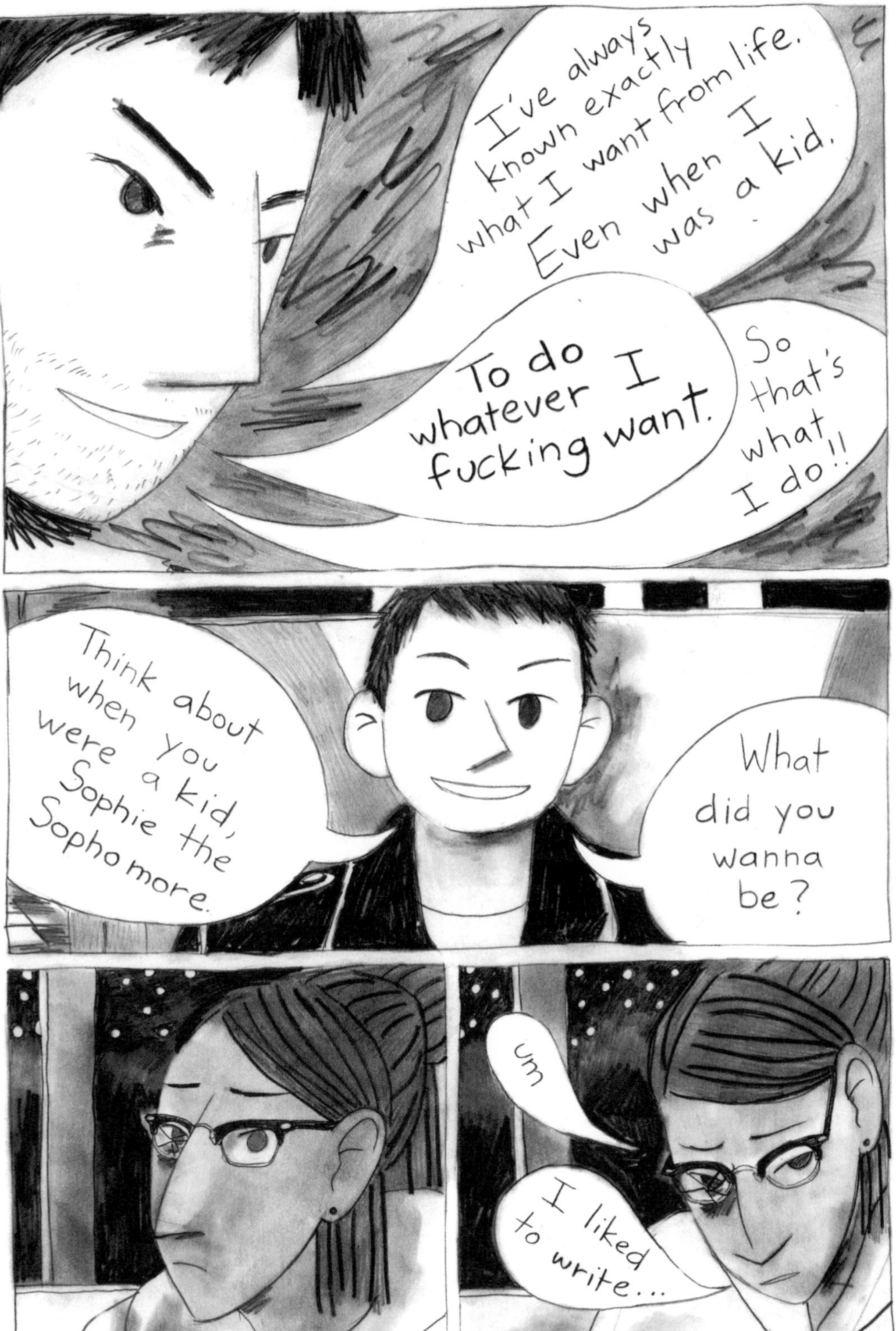
I've always known exactly what I want from life. Even when I was a kid.
To do whatever I fucking want.
So that's what I do!!
Think about when you were a kid, Sophie the Sophomore.
What did you wanna be?
um
I liked to write...

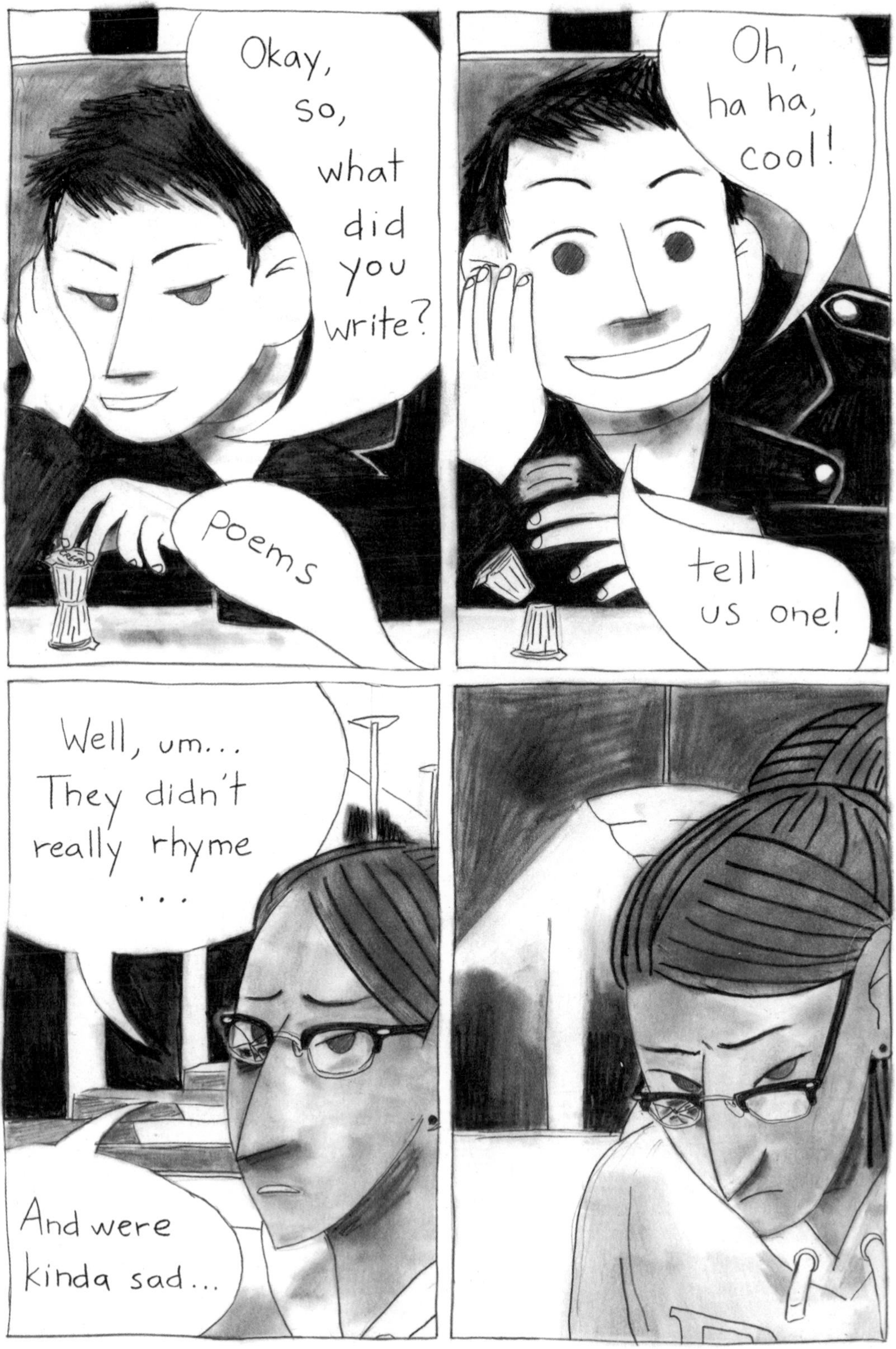
Okay, so, what did you write?
poems
Oh, ha ha, cool!
tell us one!
Well, um... They didn't really rhyme ...
And were kinda sad...

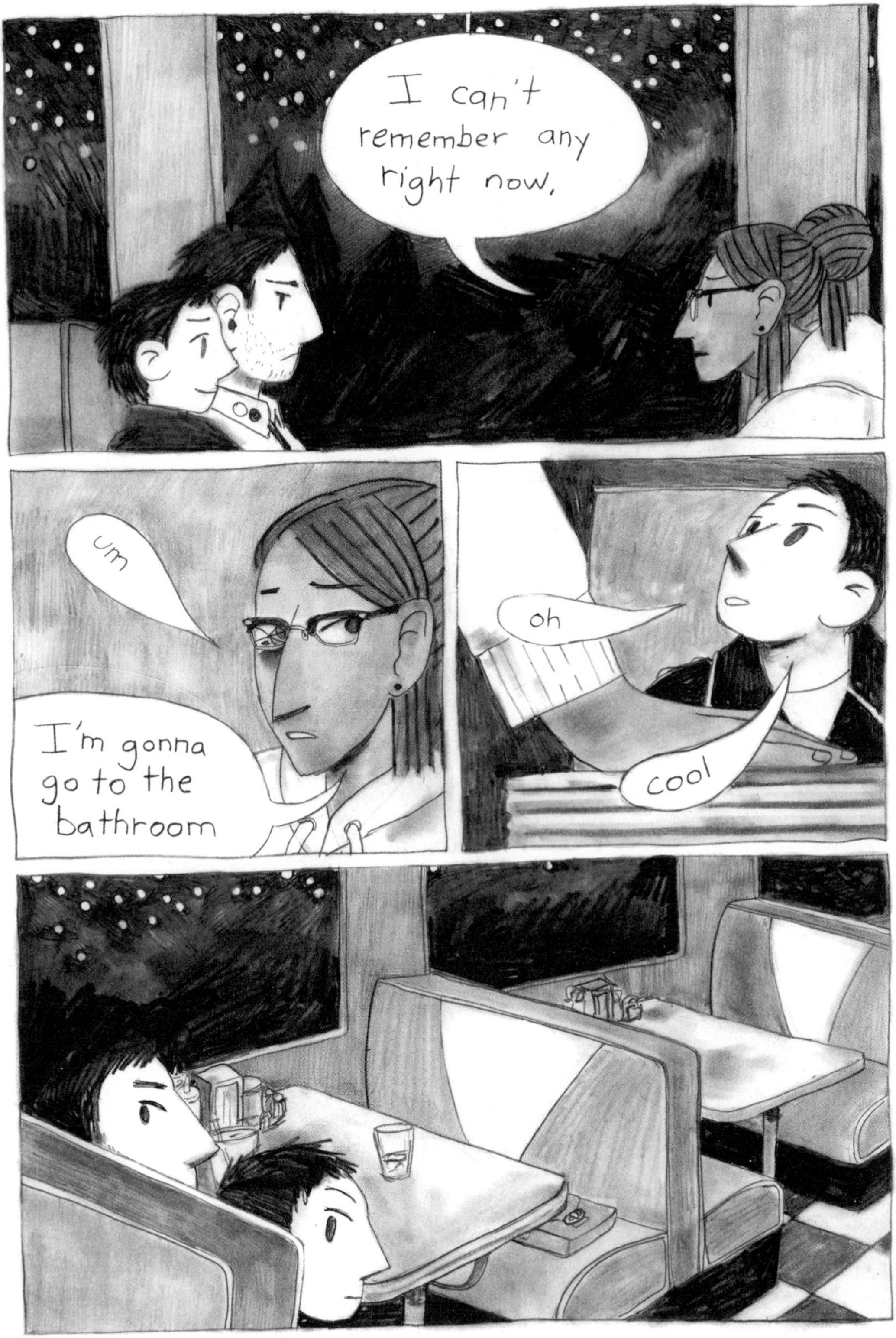
I can't remember any right now.
um
I'm gonna go to the bathroom
oh
cool

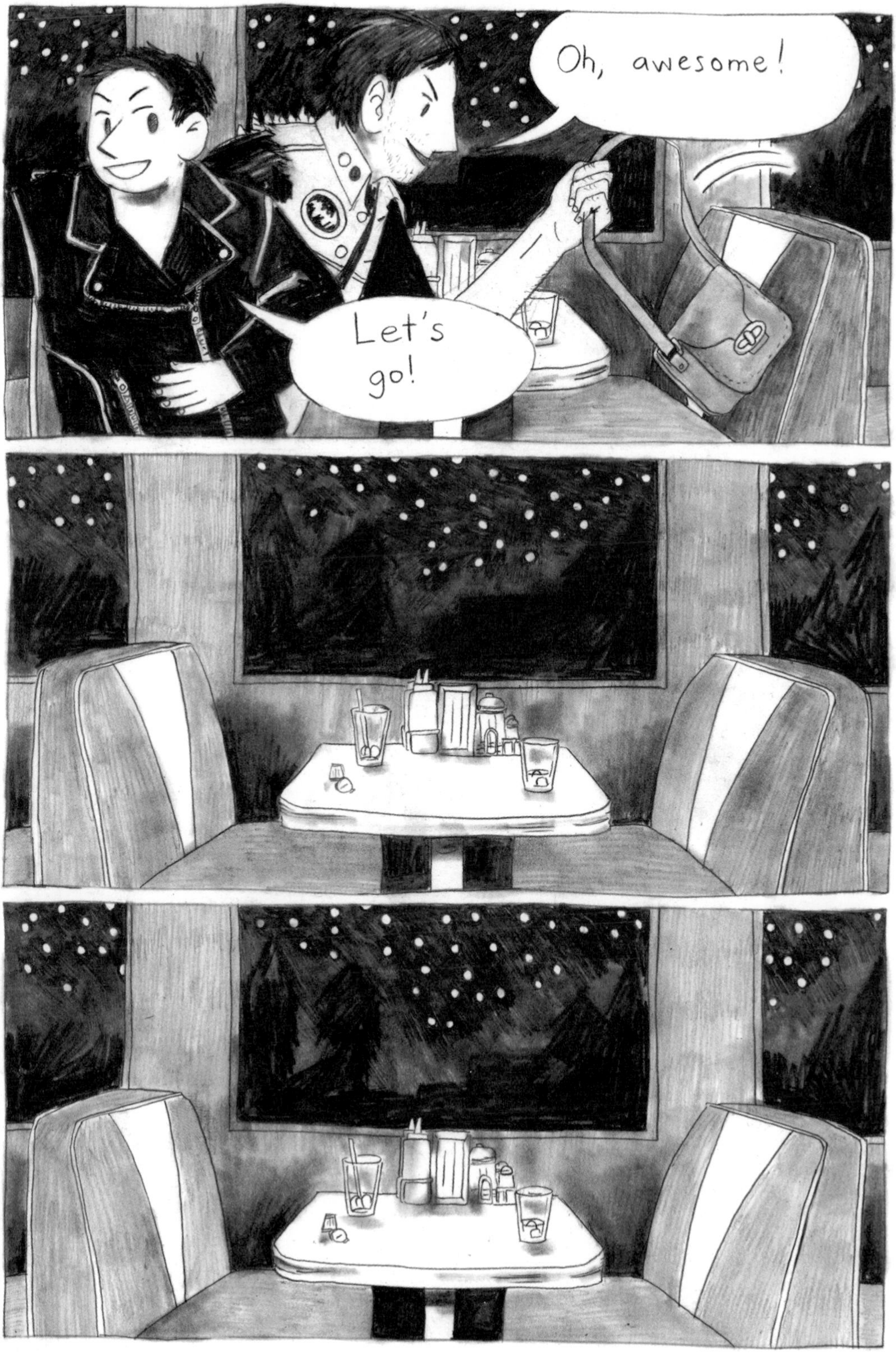
Oh, awesome!
Let's go!

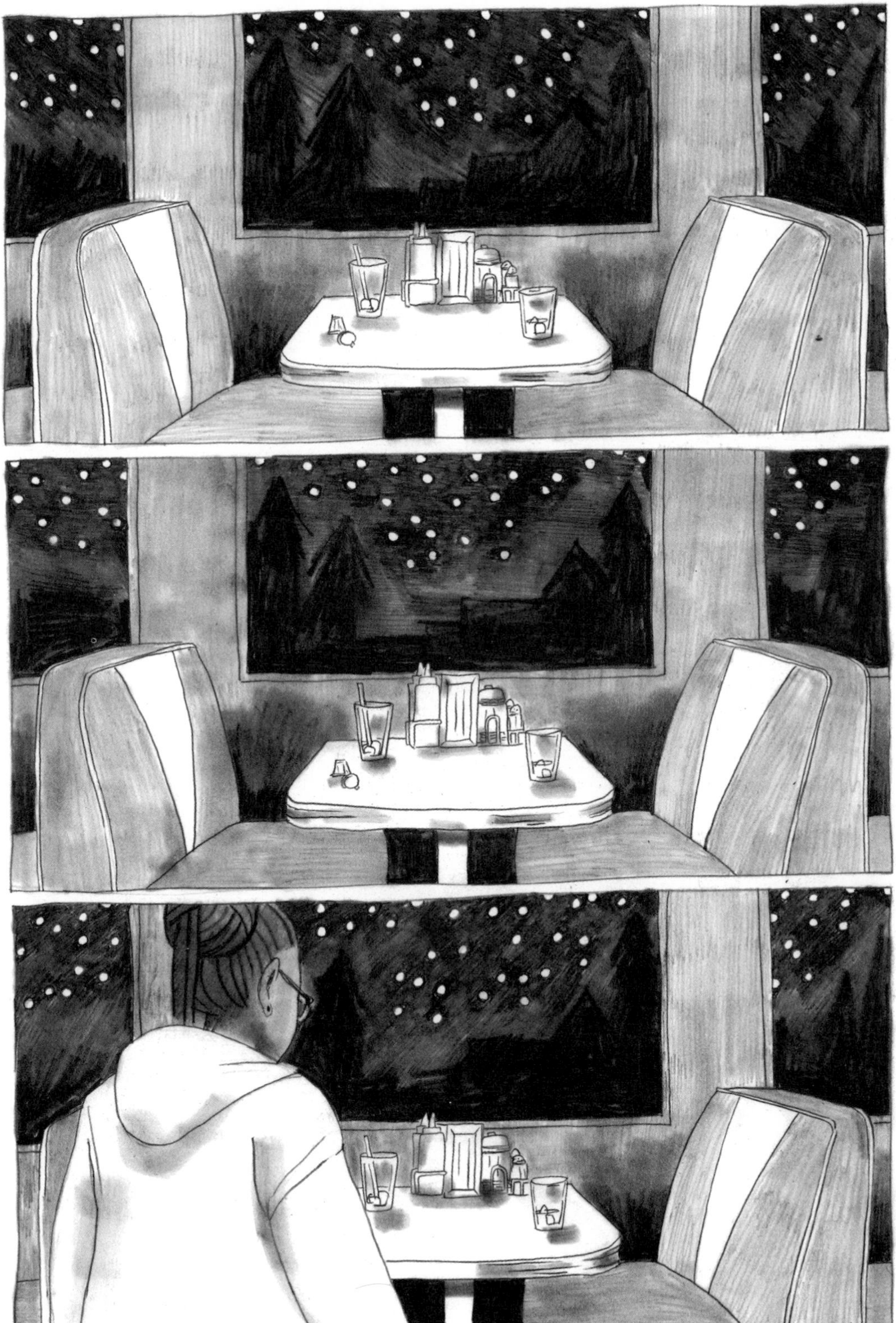

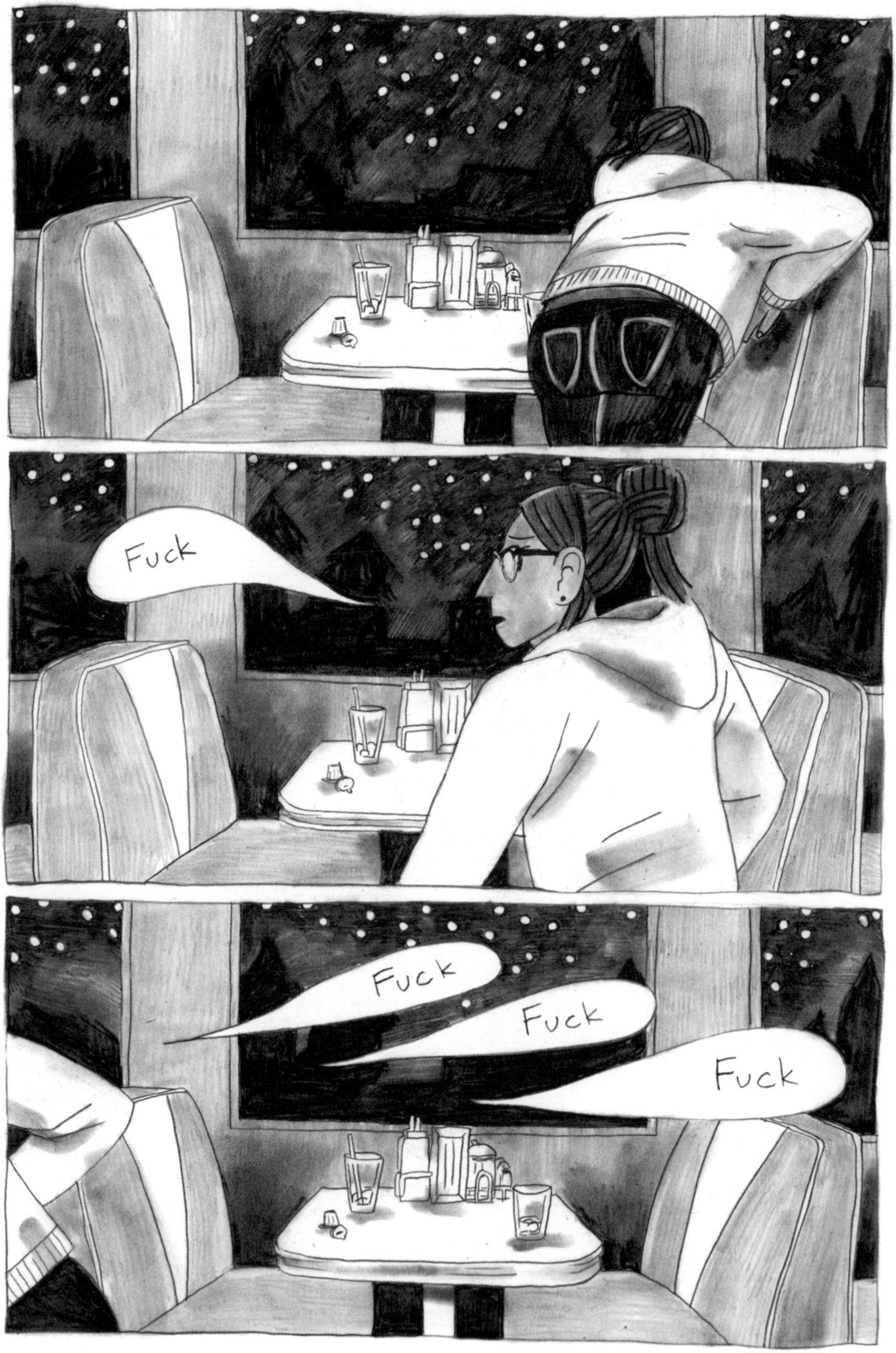
Fuck
Fuck
Fuck
Fuck

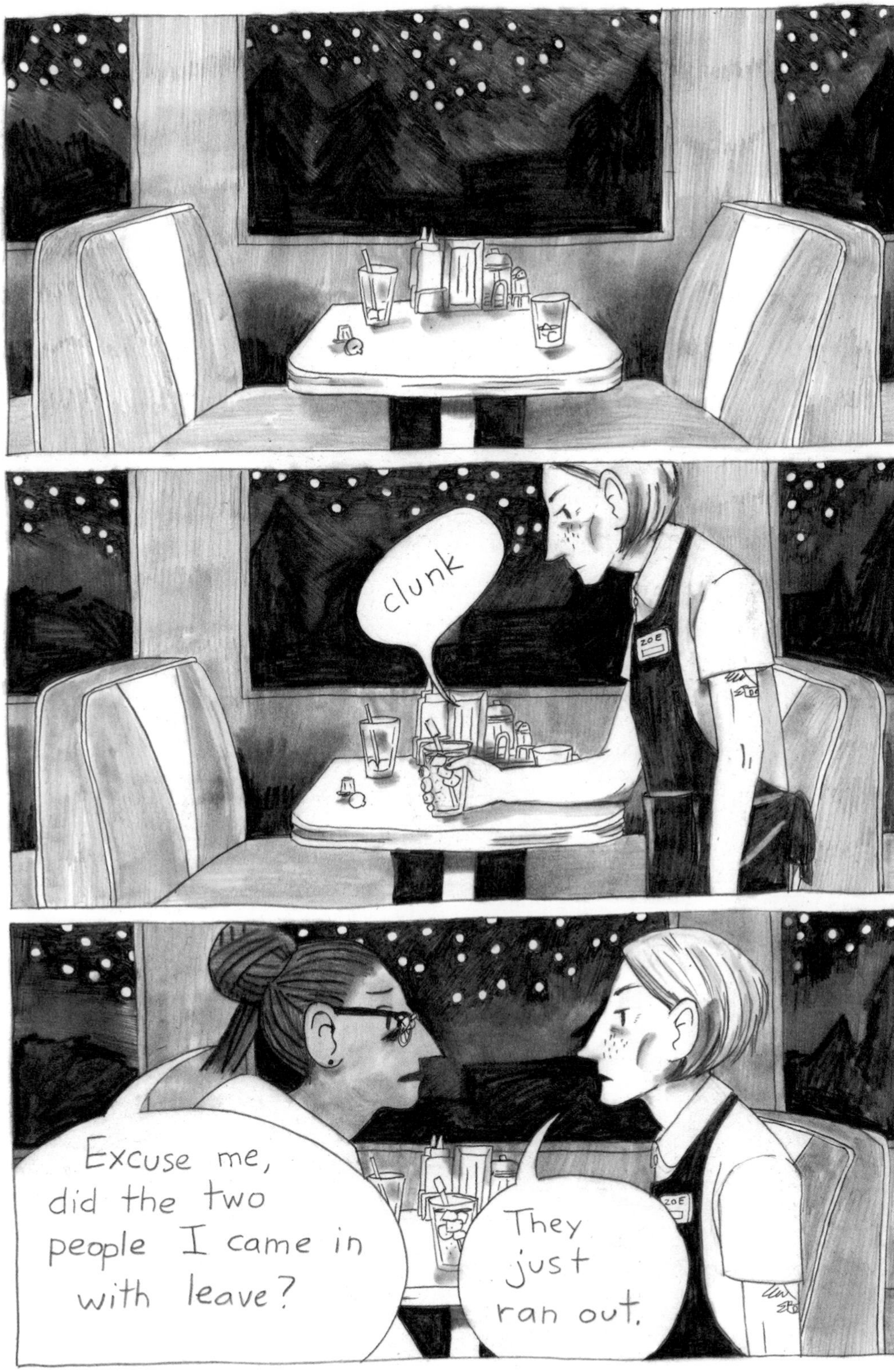
clunk
ZOE
Excuse me, did the two people I came in with leave?
They just ran out.
ZOE

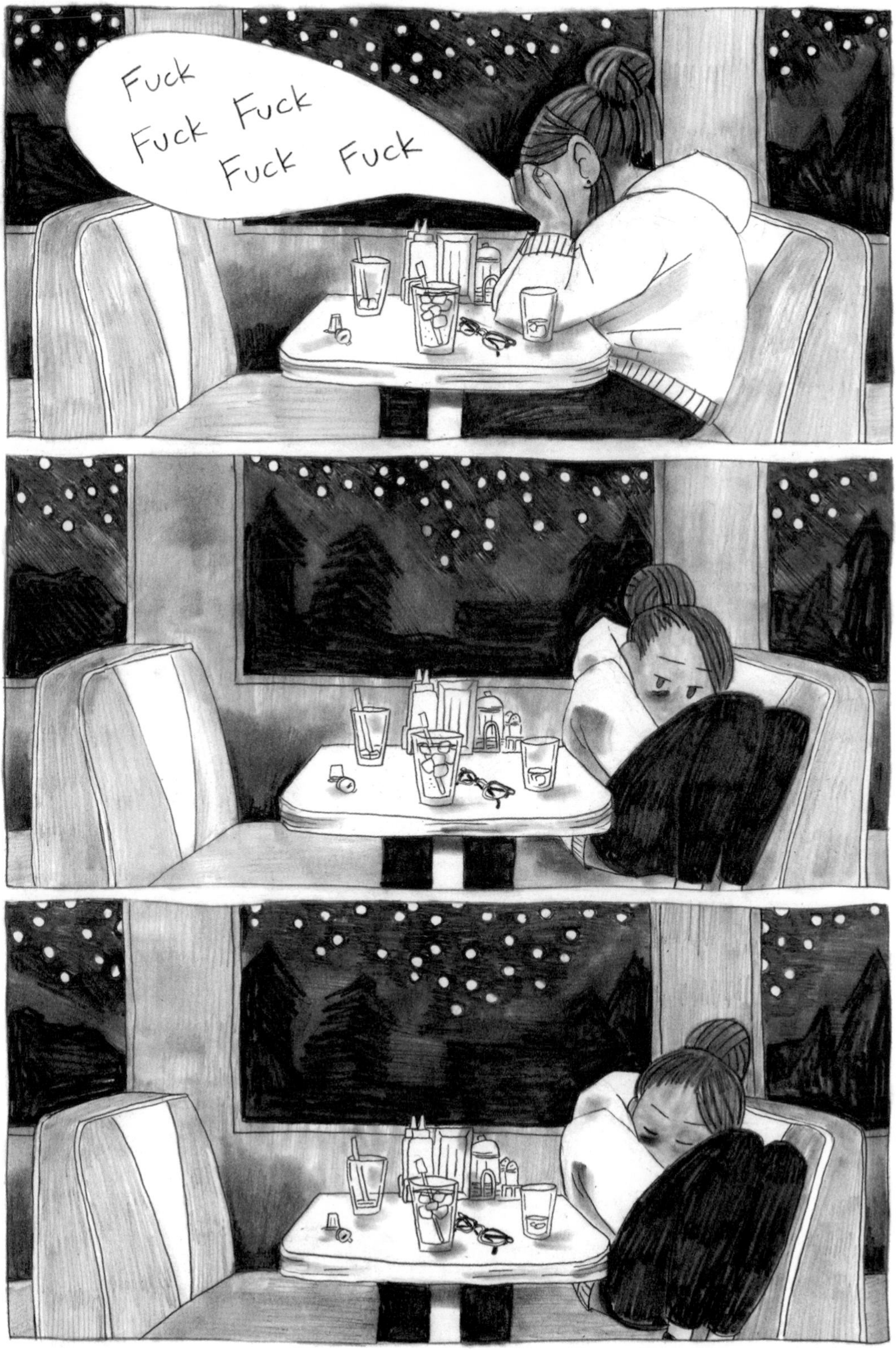
Fuck
Fuck Fuck
Fuck Fuck

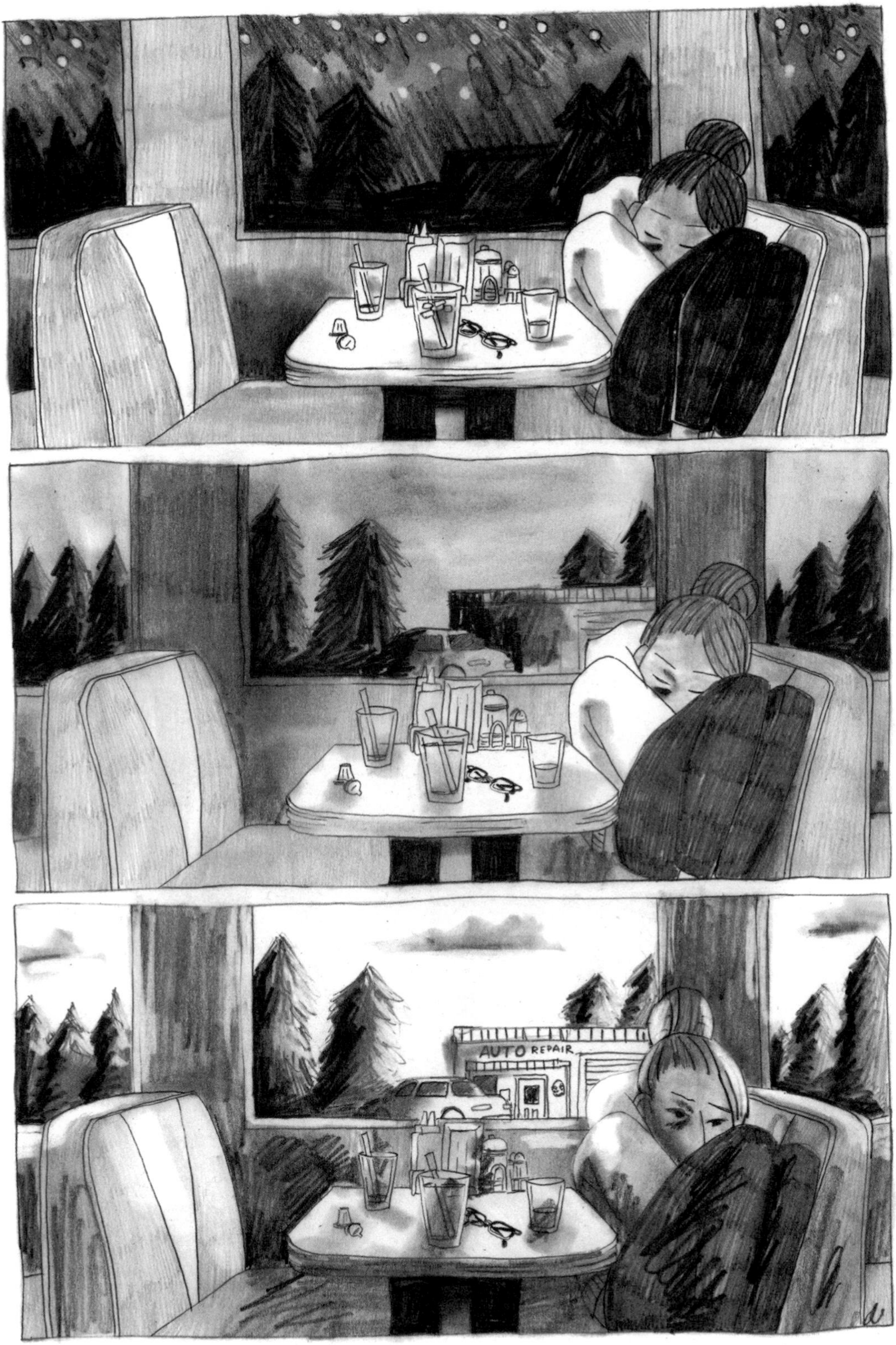
AUTO REPAIR

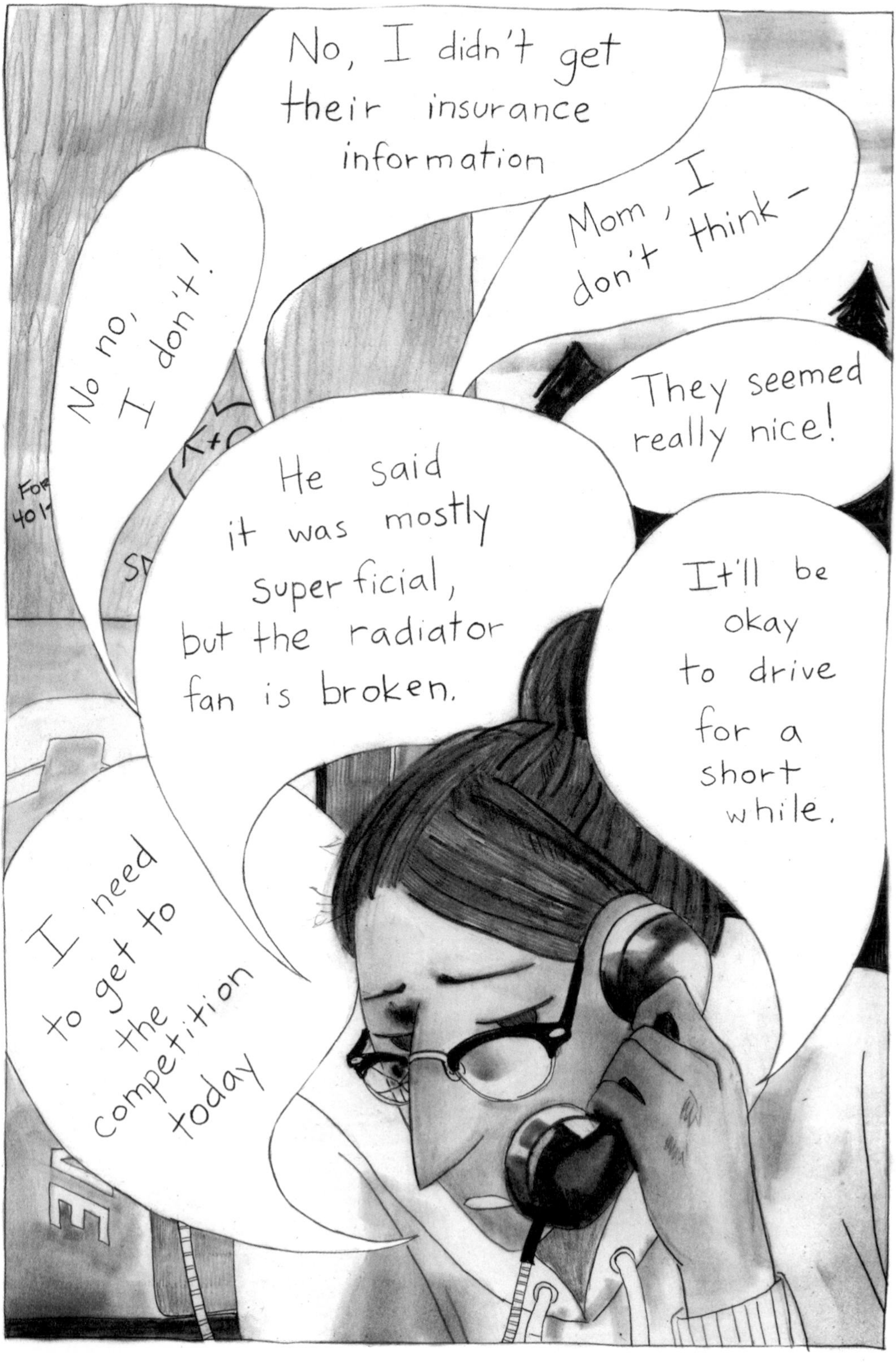
No, I didn't get their insurance information
No no, I don't!
Mom, I don't think—
They seemed really nice!
He said it was mostly superficial, but the radiator fan is broken.
It'll be okay to drive for a short while.
I need to get to the competition today

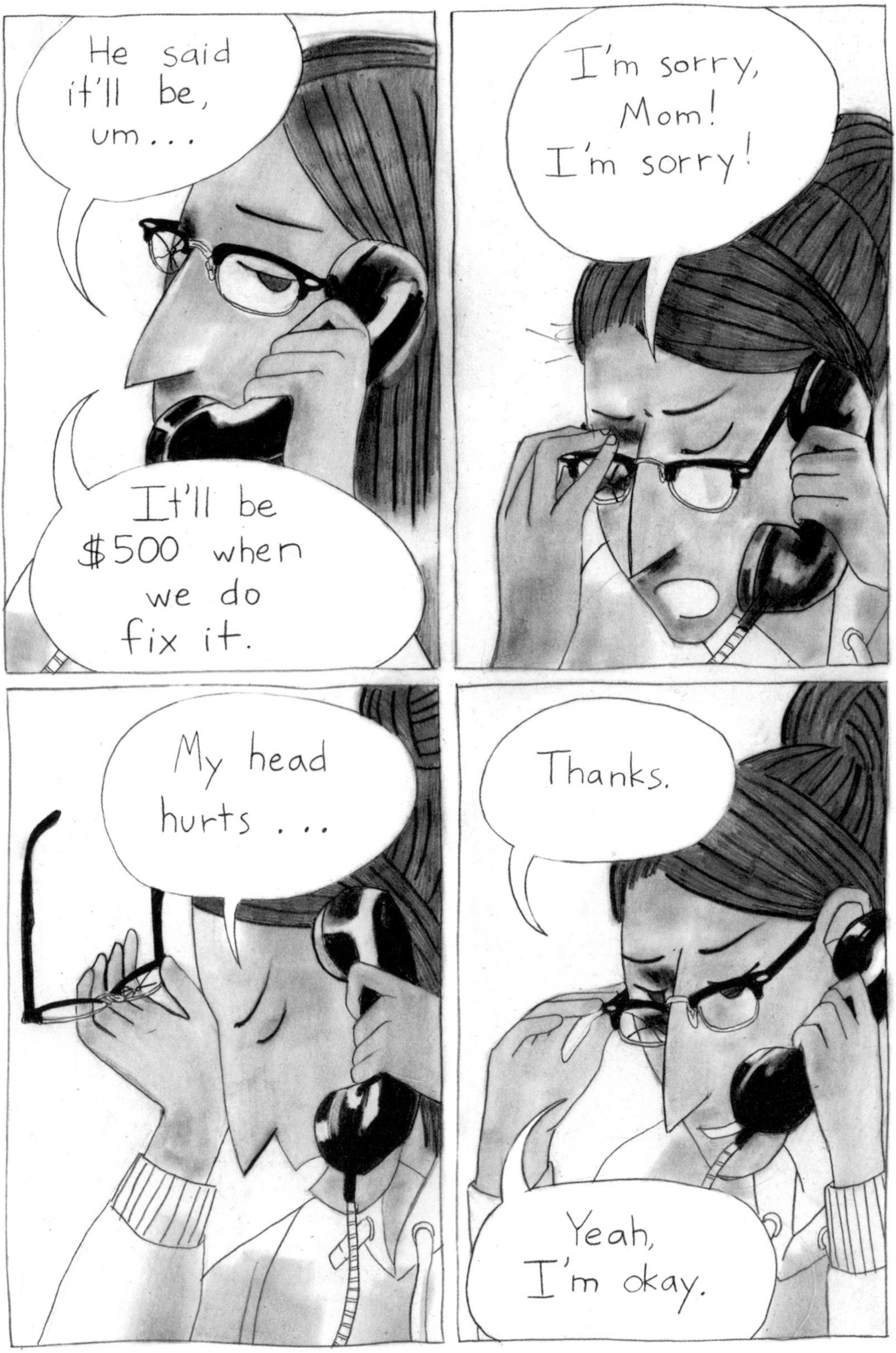
He said it'll be, um...
It'll be $500 when we do fix it.
I'm sorry, Mom! I'm sorry!
My head hurts ...
Thanks.
Yeah, I'm okay.

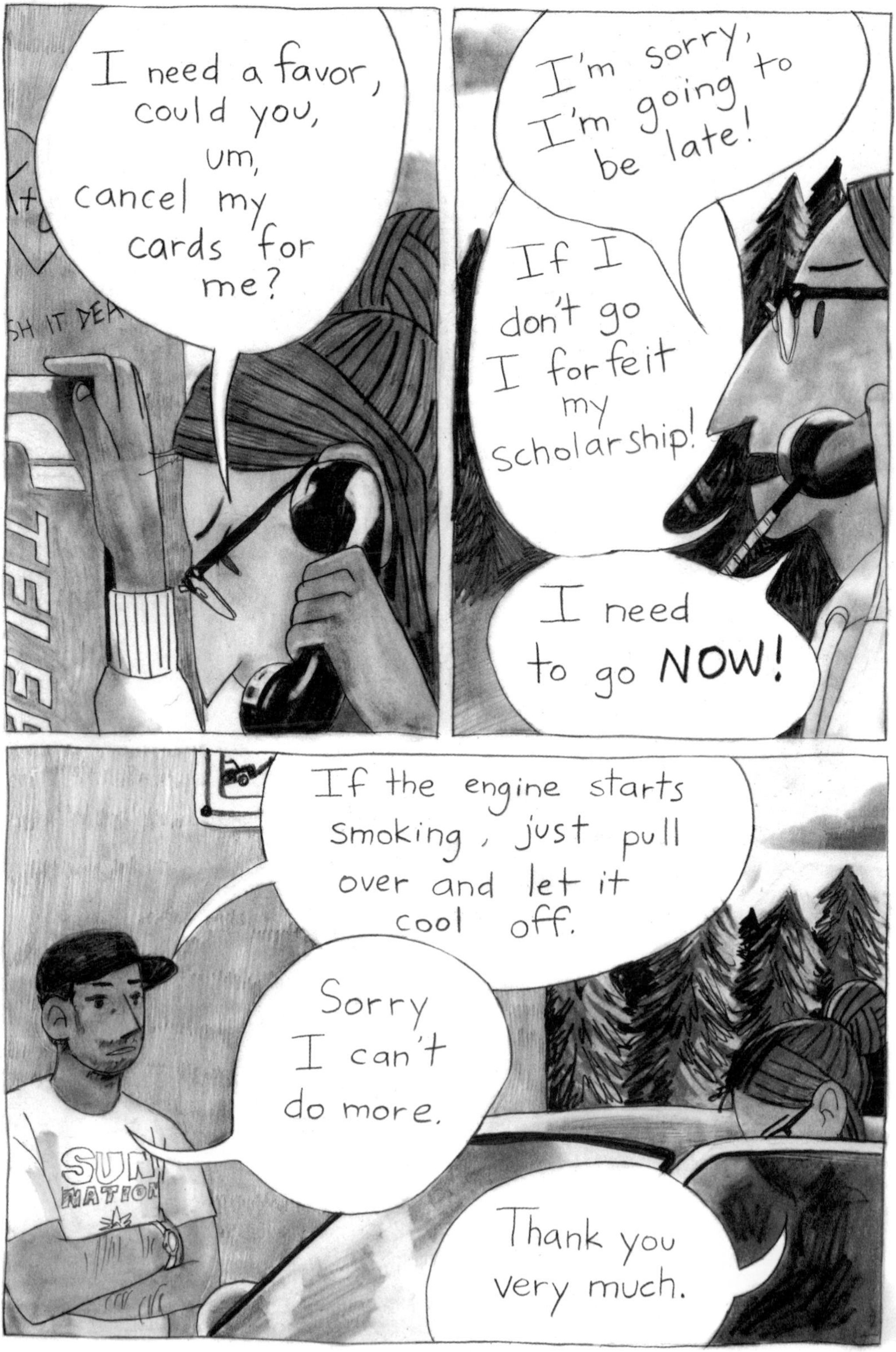
I need a favor, could you, um, cancel my cards for me?
SH IT DEA
I'm sorry, I'm going to be late!
If I don't go I forfeit my scholarship!
I need to go NOW!
If the engine starts smoking, just pull over and let it cool off.
Sorry I can't do more.
SUN NATION
Thank you very much.

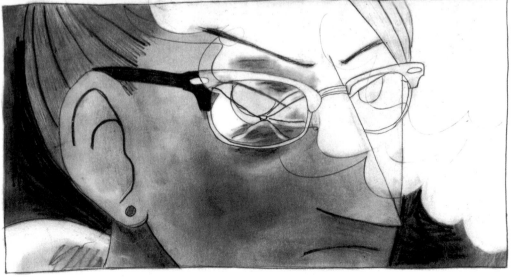

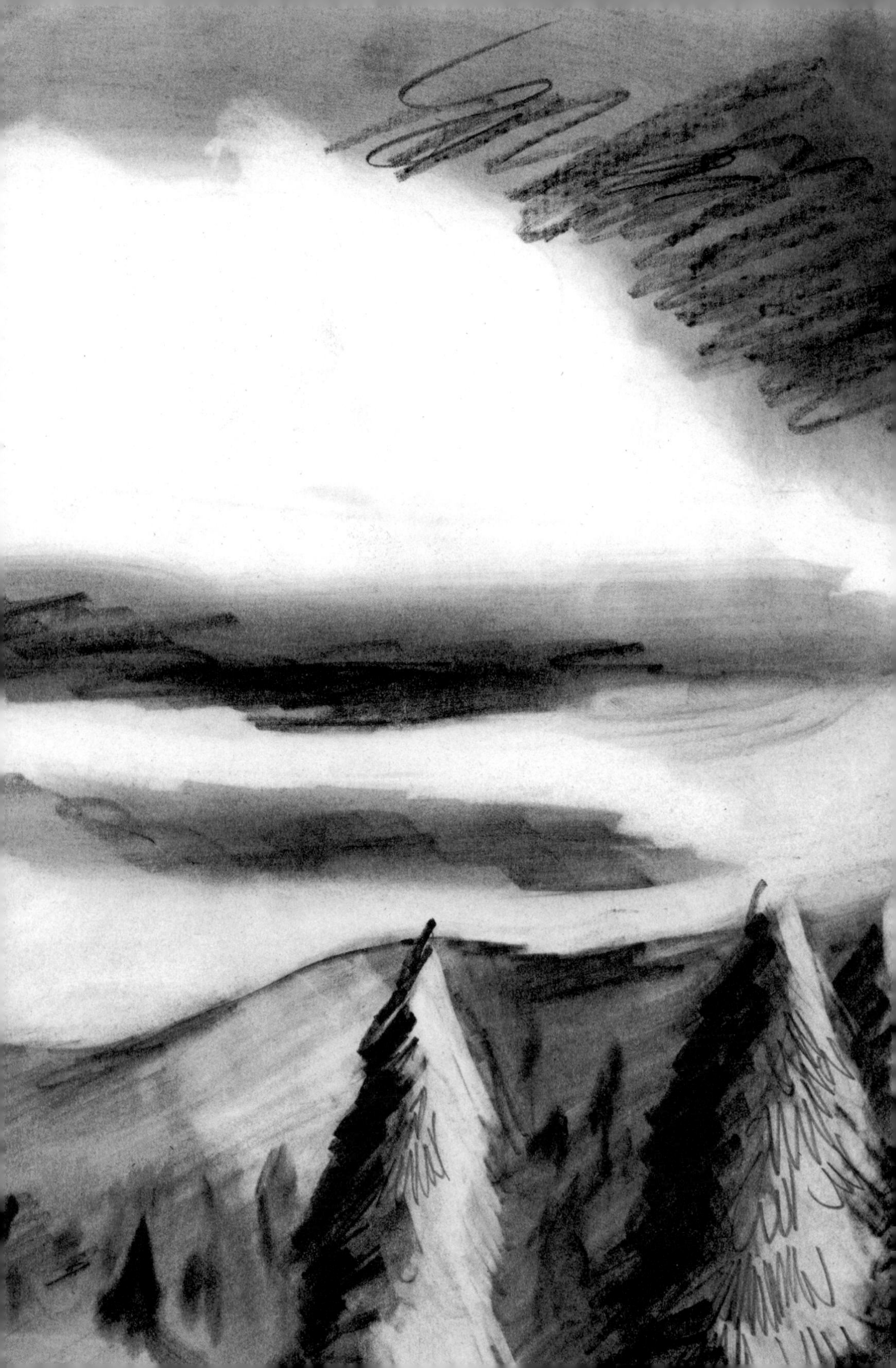

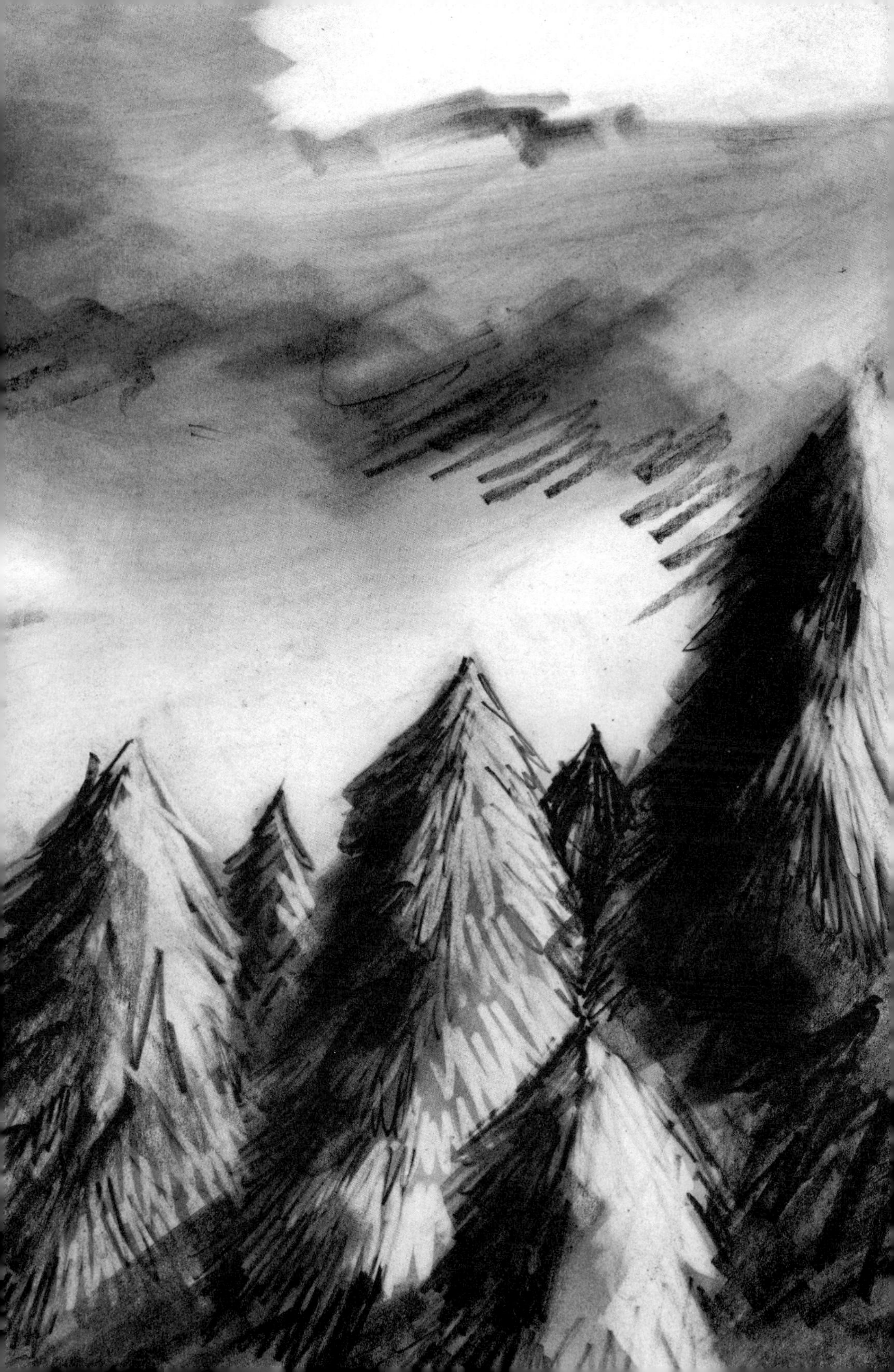

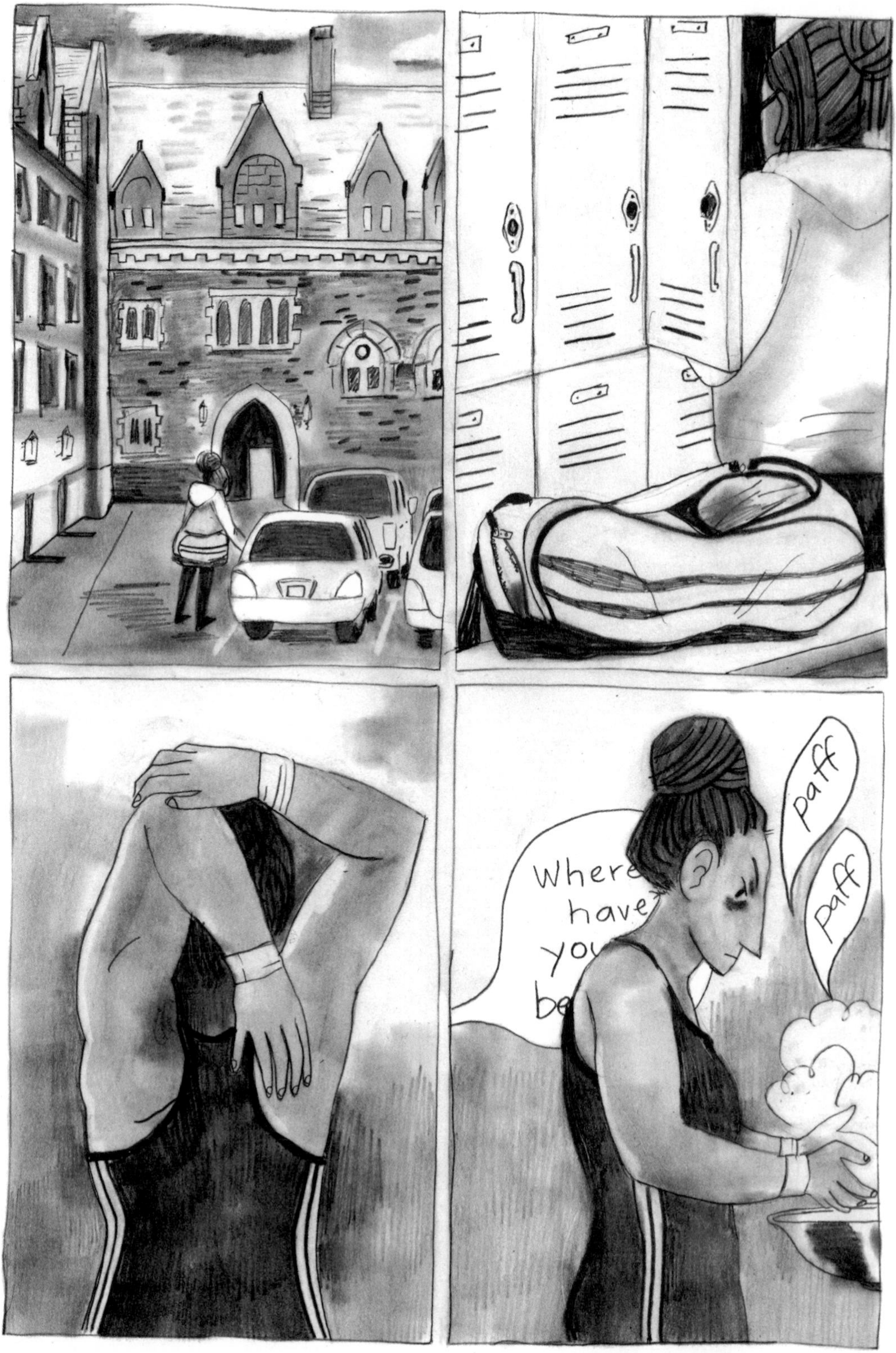
Where have you be
paff
paff

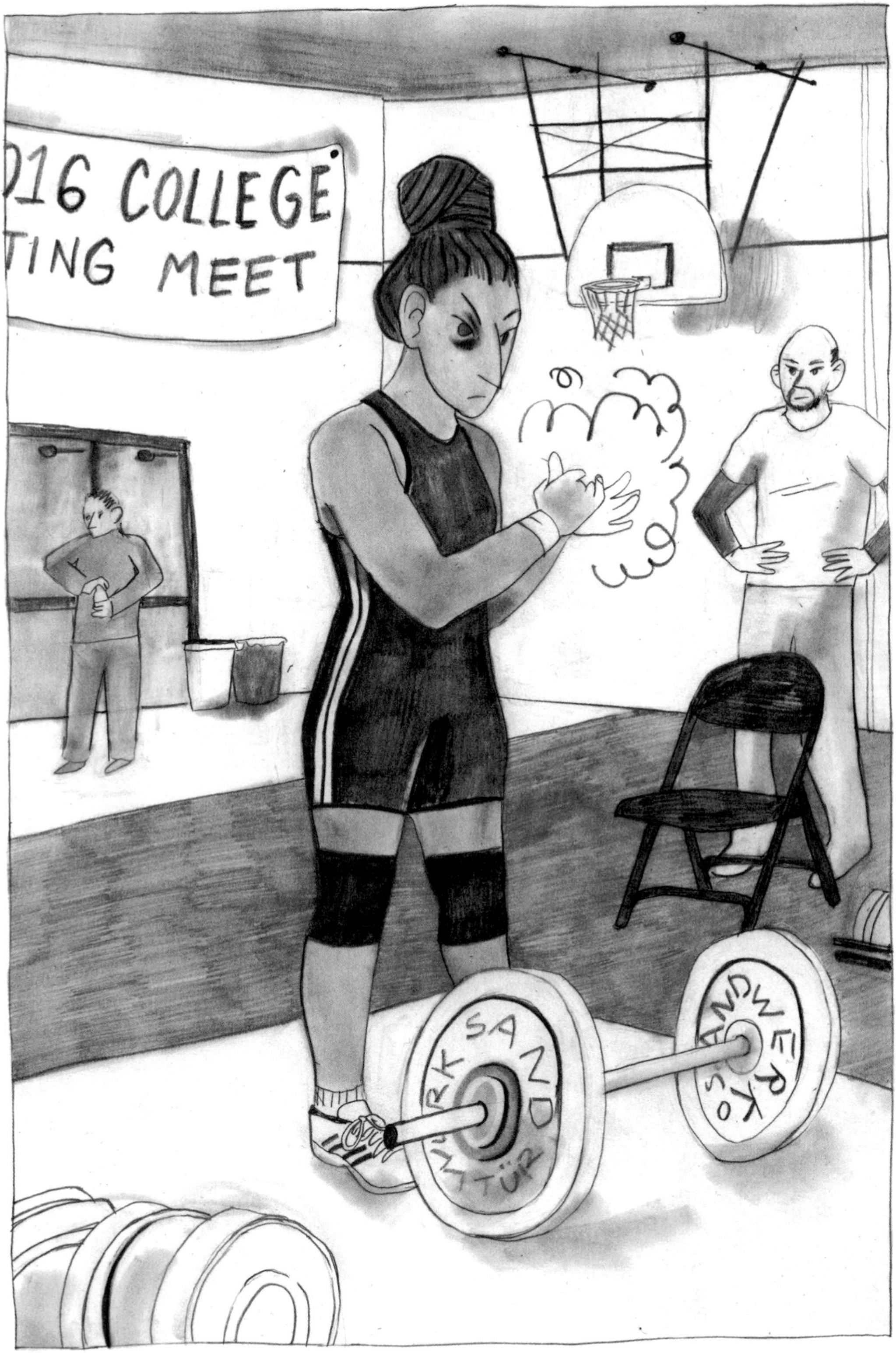

016 COLLEGE
TING MEET
WURK SANDTÜR
SANDWERKO

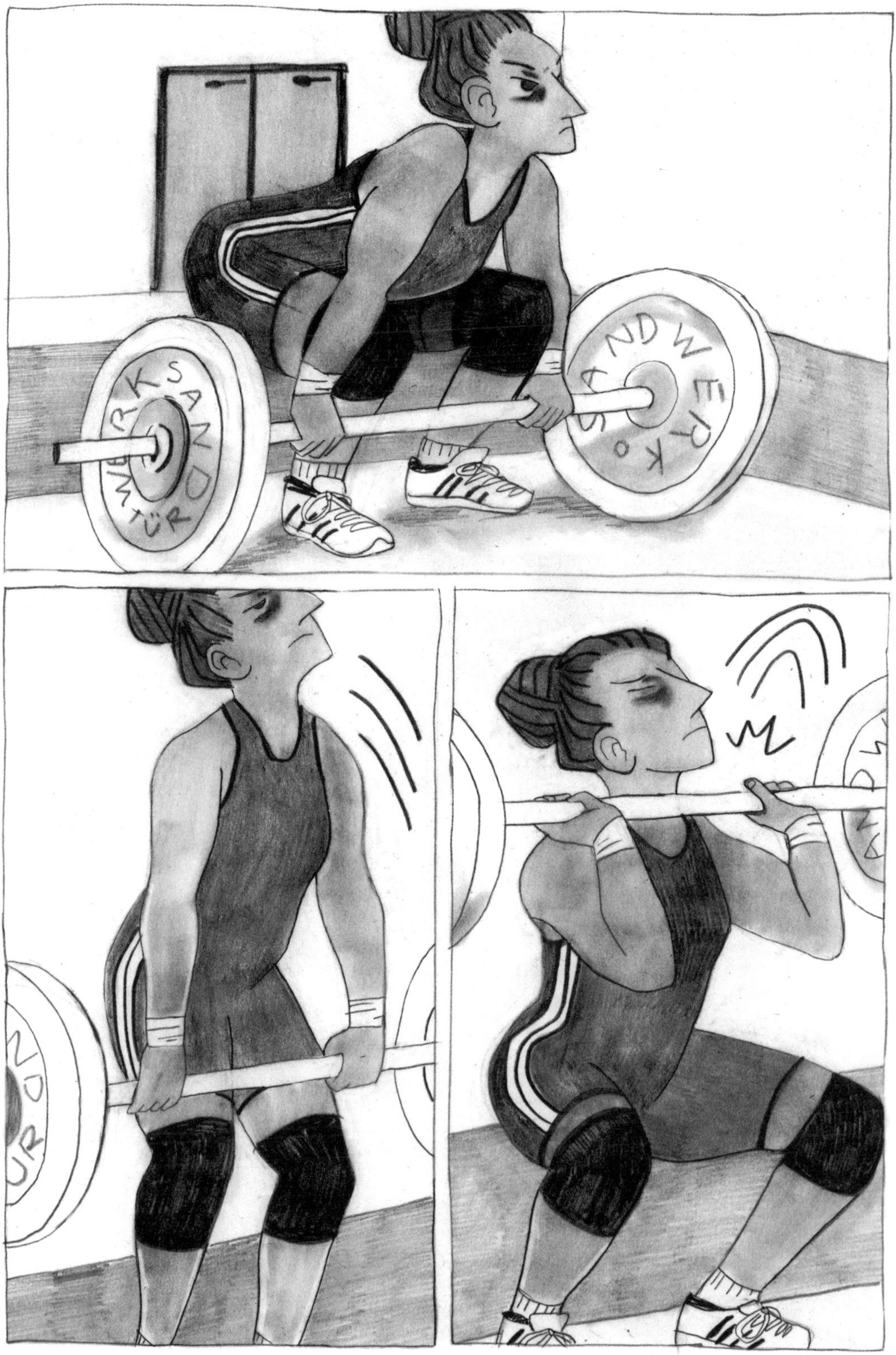

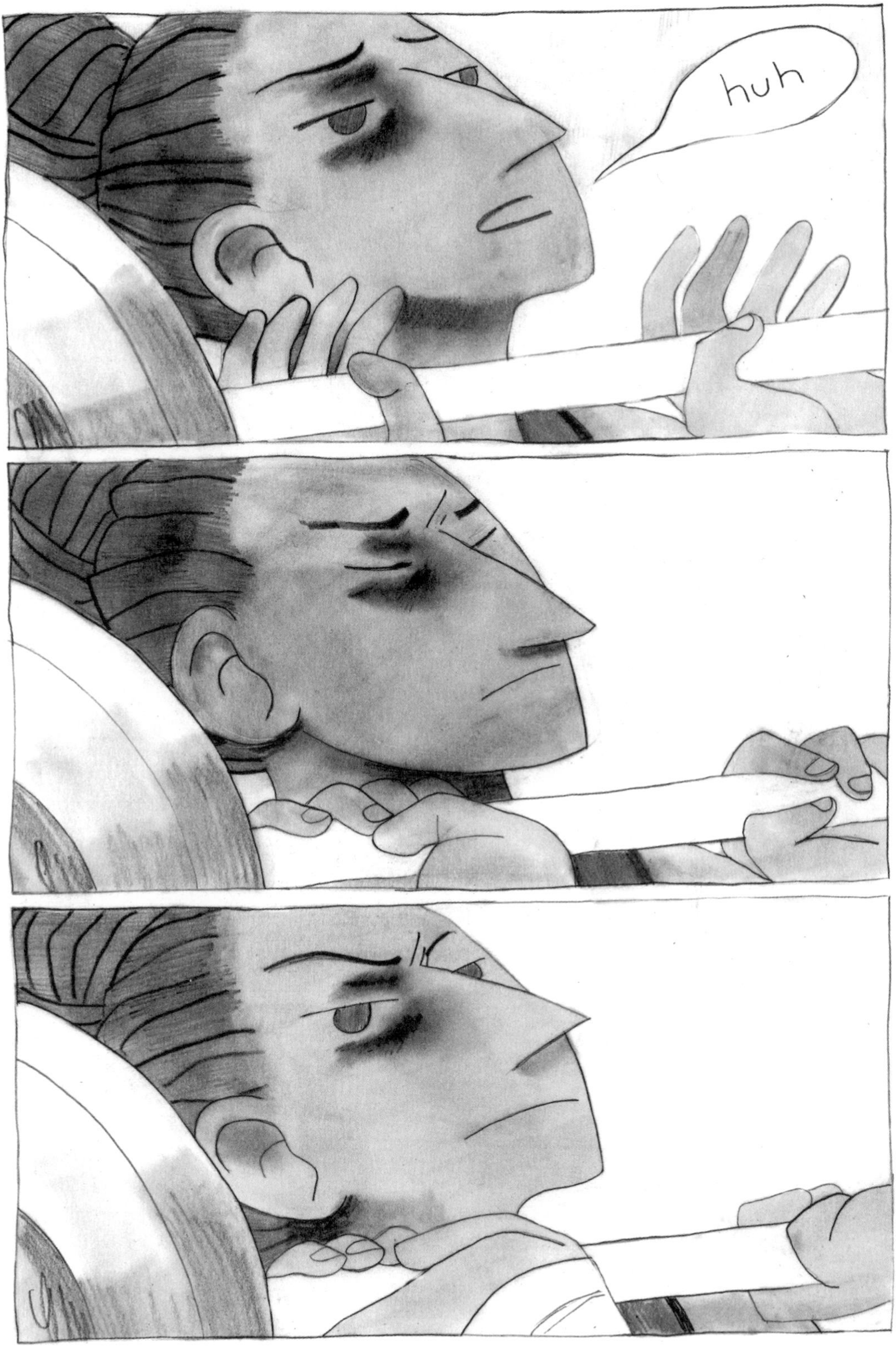
huh

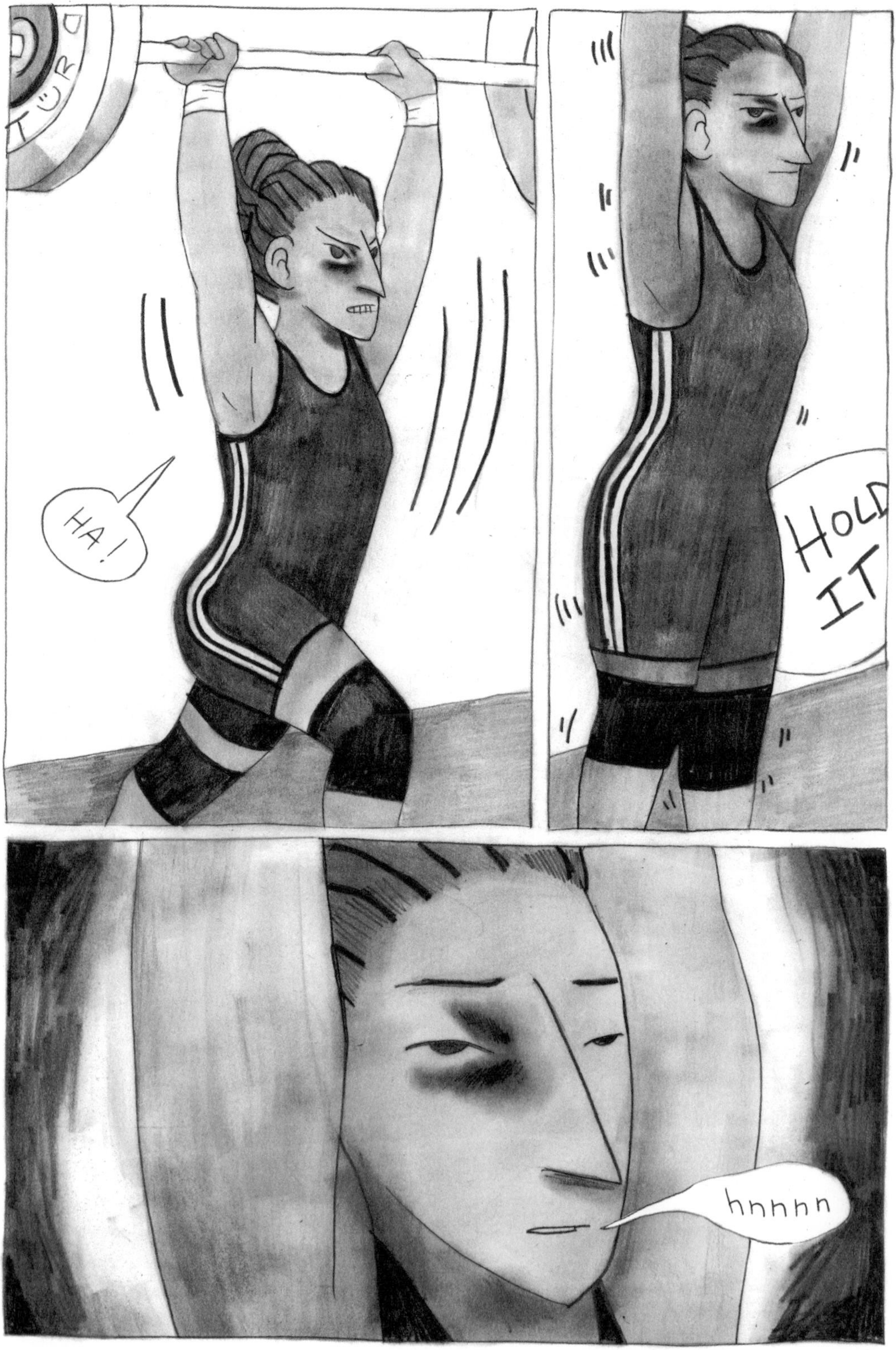
HA!
HOLD IT
hhhhh

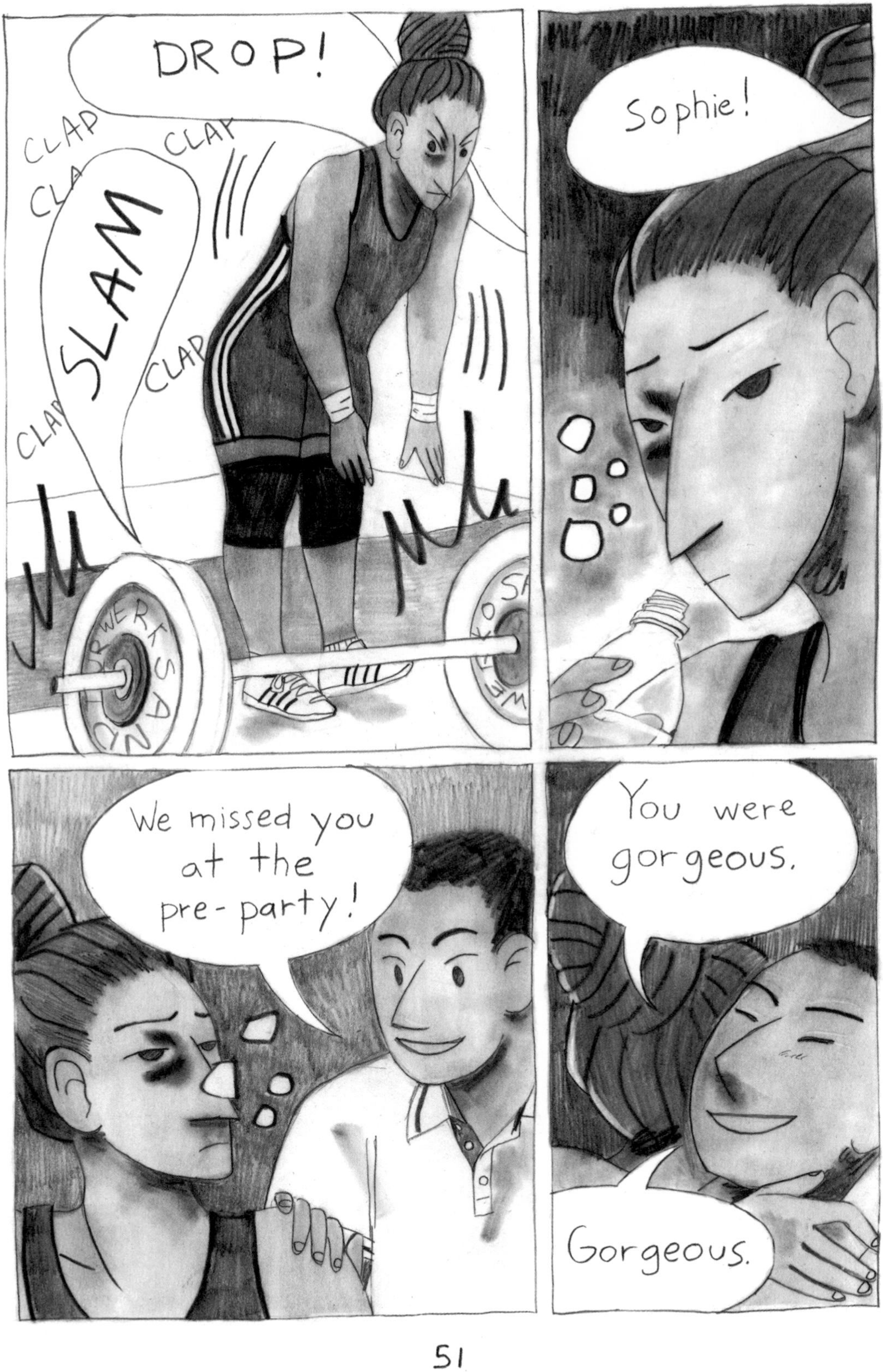
DROP!
CLAP
CLAP
CLAP
SLAM
CLAP
CLAP
WERKSANDUR
Sophie!
We missed you at the pre-party!
You were gorgeous.
Gorgeous.

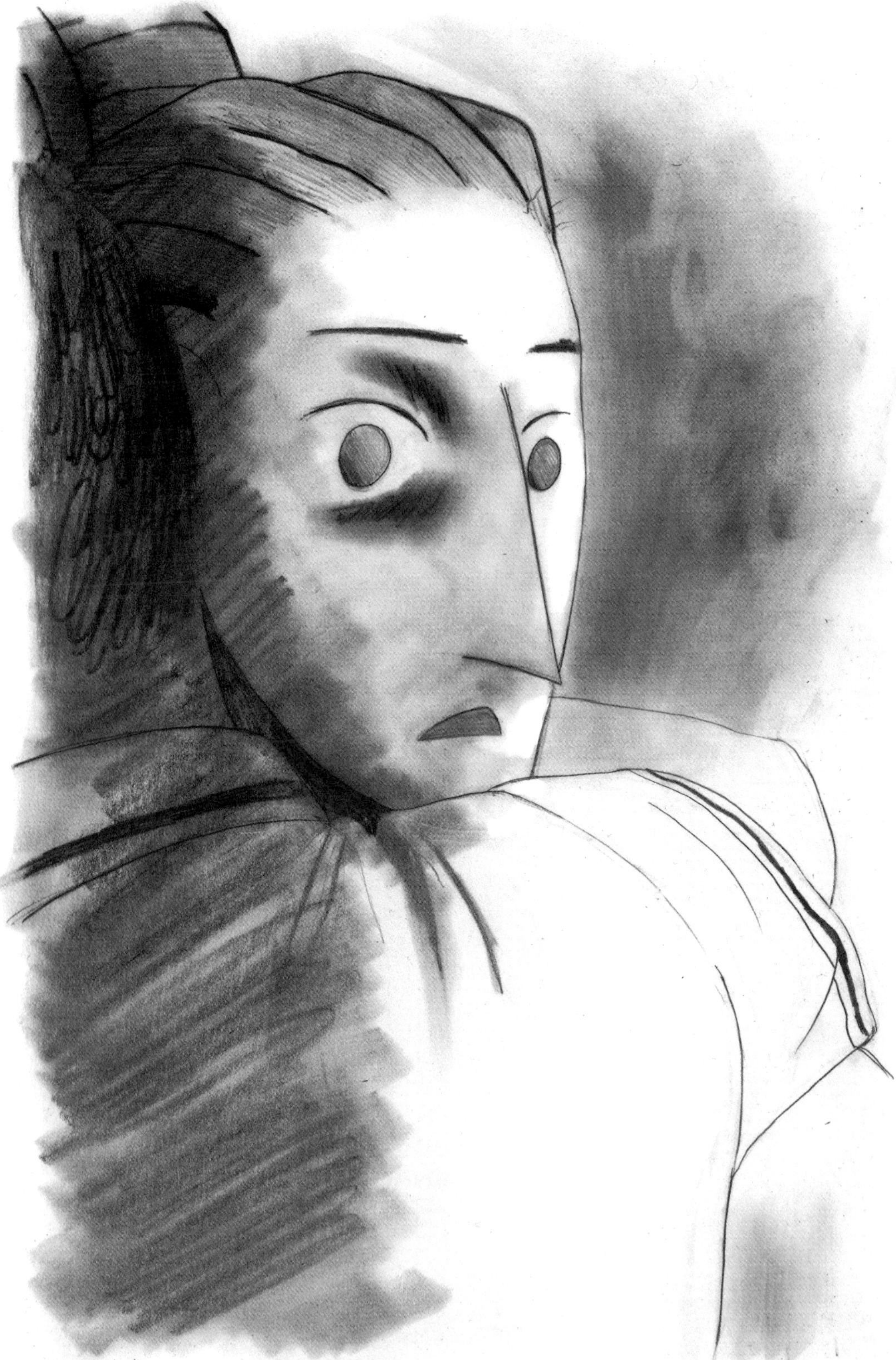

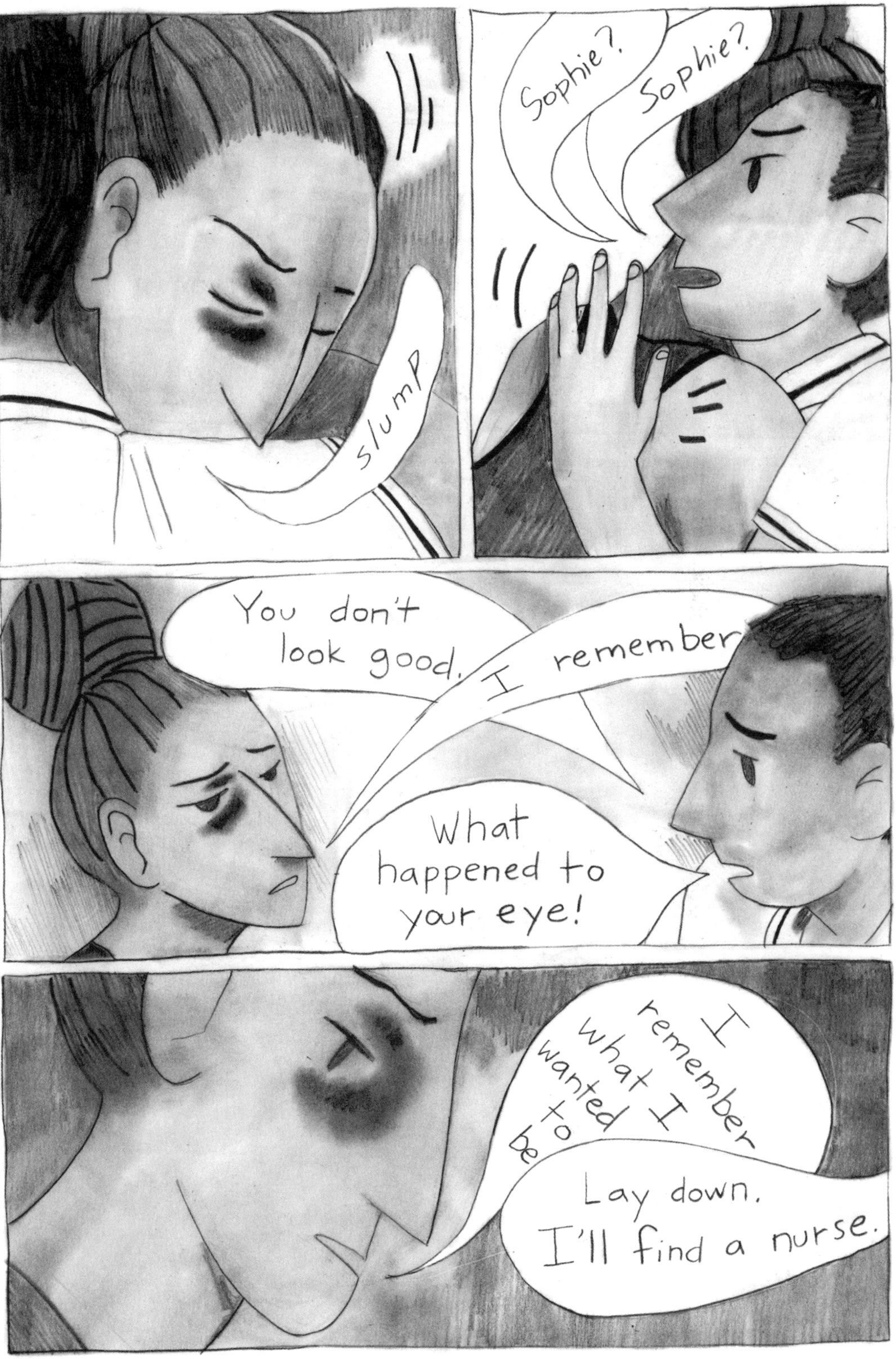
slump
Sophie? Sophie?
You don't look good.
I remember
What happened to your eye!
I remember what I wanted to be
Lay down. I'll find a nurse.

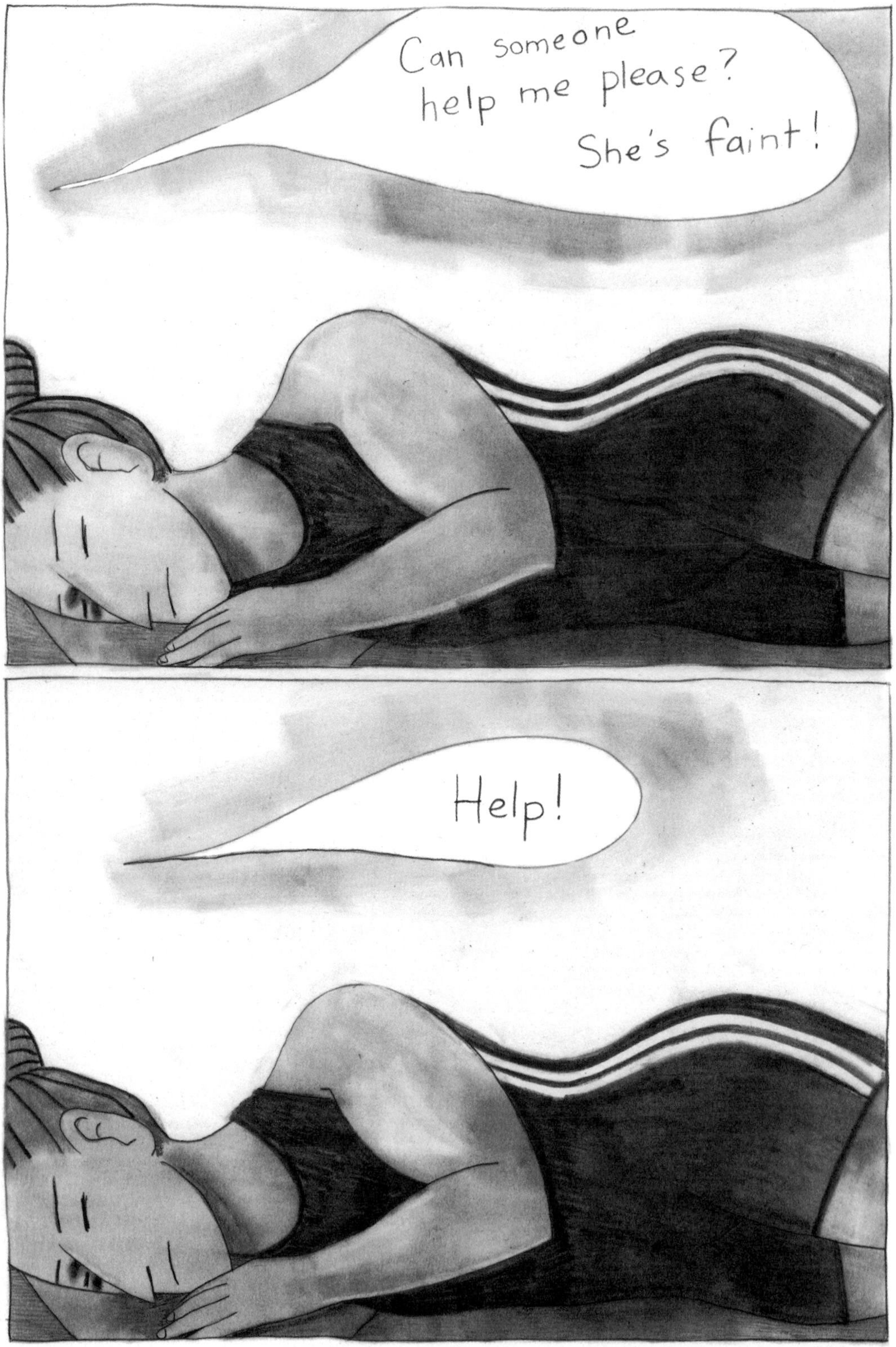
Can someone help me please? She's faint!
Help!

I remember what
I wanted to be
as a kid

Shooting stars
are ghosts
going to heaven

Someday
I want to be
a shooting star

Gorgeous
A poem by Sophie Azul

11 years old

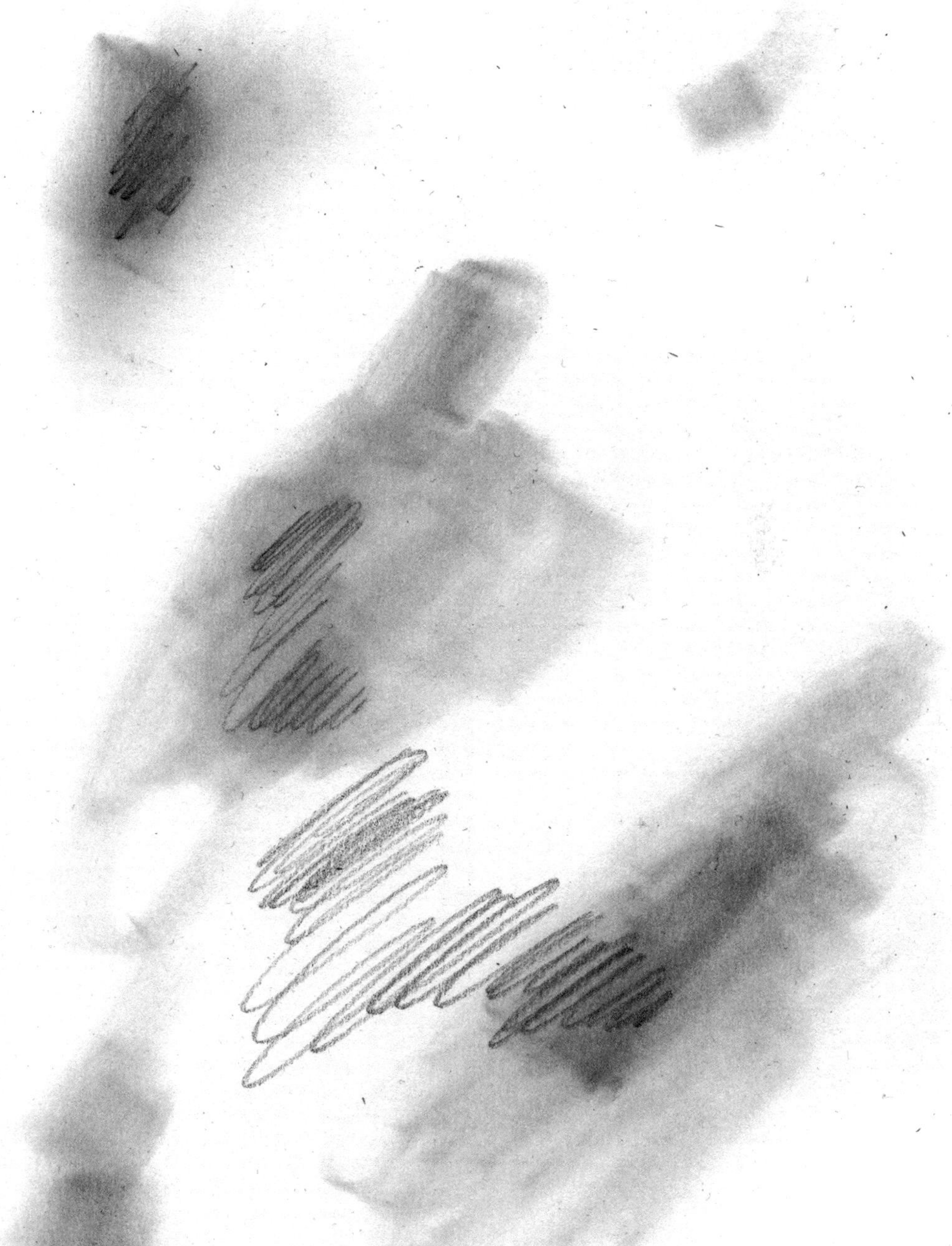

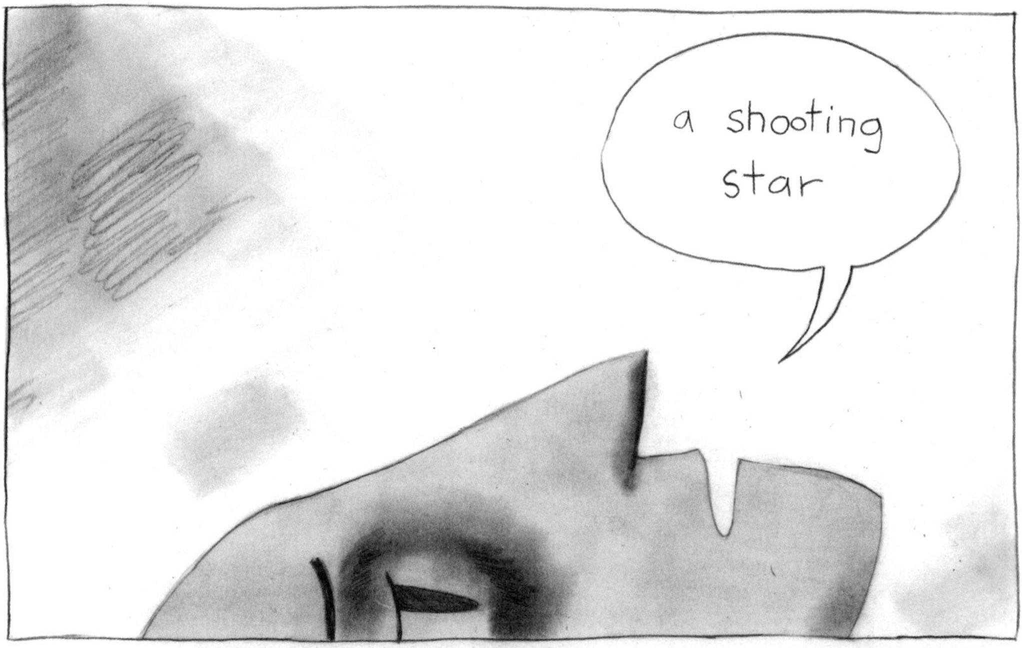
a shooting star

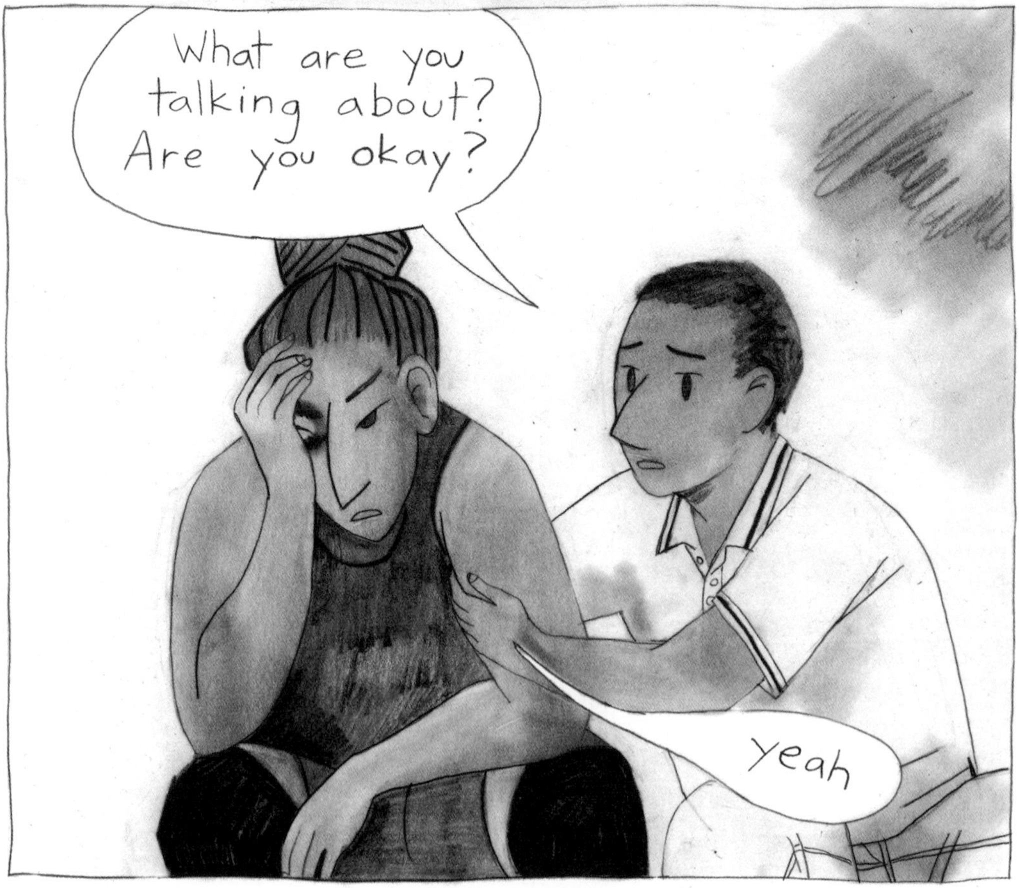
What are you talking about? Are you okay?
yeah

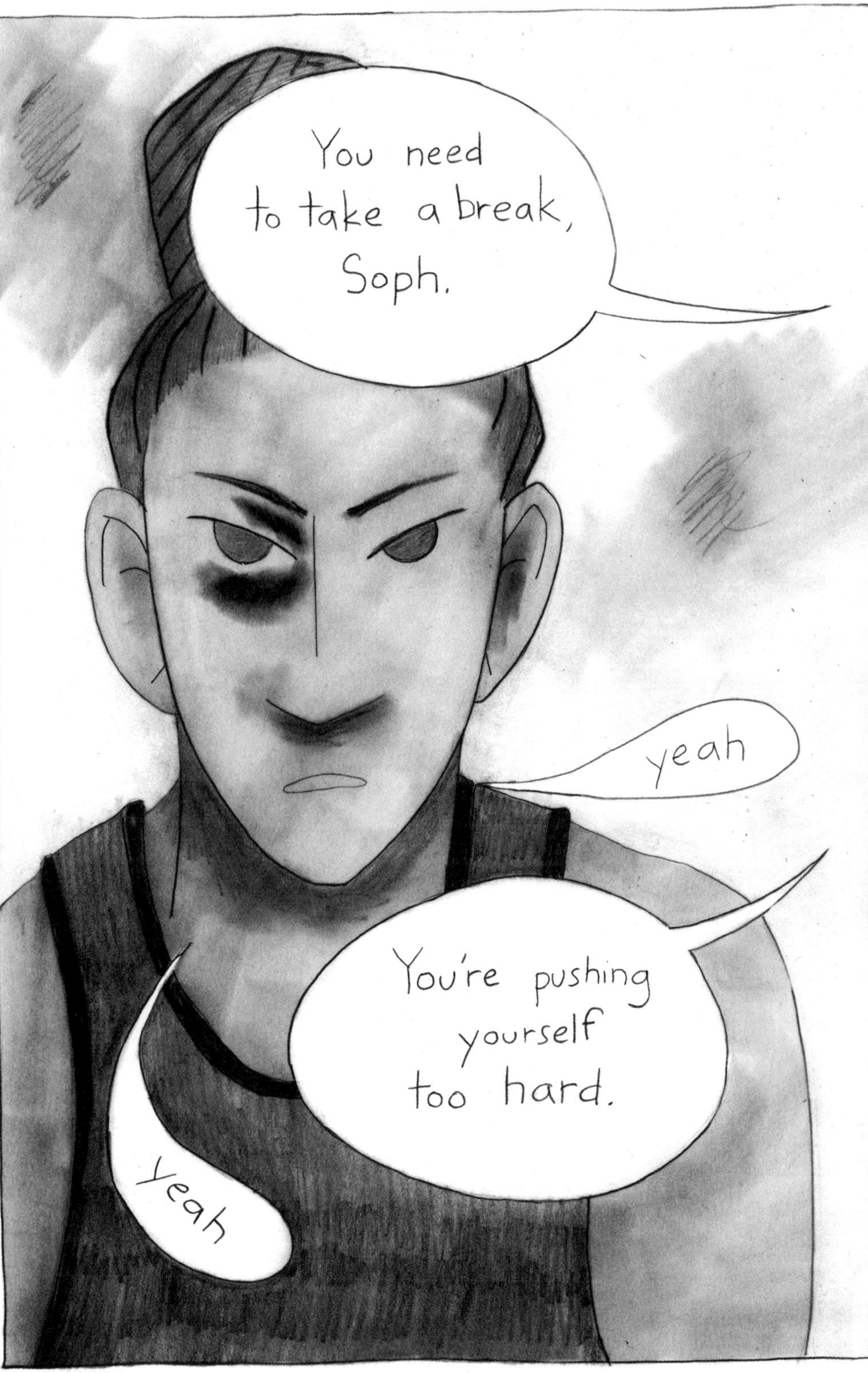
You need to take a break, Soph.
yeah
You're pushing yourself too hard.
yeah

Cathy G. Johnson is an artist
in Providence, Rhode Island.
She grew up in Minnesota and
graduated from the Maryland Institute
College of Art in 2011.
She won the 2014 Ignatz Award
for most promising new talent.